ACROSS THE WORLD IN A
Moggie!
LONDON-TO-MELBOURNE BY ROAD

ACROSS THE WORLD IN A Moggie!

LONDON TO MELBOURNE BY ROAD

VAL WILKINSON

ATHENA PRESS
LONDON

ACROSS THE WORLD IN A MOGGIE!
London to Melbourne by Road
Copyright © Val Wilkinson 2008

All Rights Reserved

ISBN: 978 1 84748 391 1

First published 2008 by
ATHENA PRESS
Queen's House, 2 Holly Road
Twickenham TW1 4EG
United Kingdom

Printed for Athena Press

Thanks to:
my friend Pam for her technical support;
my sons – Aidan for his encouragement to write this book,
Aaron for his cover design;
and to Graham for reminding me of incidents that I had forgotten.

Contents

Introduction

HOW NAÏVE WE WERE! WE STILL HAVE THE MAPS WITH SMALL, ballpoint crosses marked on them, showing the places where we had already decided we would be spending the night! Each was a sensible distance from the last, a reasonable day's travel, sharing the driving between the two of us. Looking back, we laughed at how simple we had tried to make it. But we thought we had planned very well, as well as you could from a distance with limited local knowledge, but with the enthusiasm of youth to tackle the unknown.

We made the trip successfully, with few mishaps. It was mulled over in the dark, English winter evenings for many years after. So why write about it now? It remains a vivid memory for both of us; memories shared with family and old friends to this day, thirty-plus years later – did we ever tell you about the floods in India? But we also made new friends on that trip, some individuals and families from different cultures with whom we still keep in contact. Another reason for writing: could such an adventure be experienced now by an ordinary young couple in their twenties? Given the current political situation in the world, how would we feel if our son and his wife wanted to drive themselves 12,000 miles, travelling through the countries we tackled without fear of kidnapping or terrorism – all because our vehicle carried a GB sticker on the back? If we said our answer to the question makes us feel sad, you can perhaps guess what we decided. Nevertheless, we hope you can enjoy and share this trip from the comfort and safety of your home.

Planning and Preparation

A VISIT FROM AN AUSTRALIAN COUPLE, ALONG WITH THEIR two children, set the idea in motion. They transported their long wheelbase Land Rover and themselves by ship to England, staying at our London home. Their plan was to drive themselves back to Oz via Africa after seeing a little of the UK and Europe (they eventually completed the trip successfully, but that's another story). Their enthusiasm inspired us to consider driving when we next visited Graham's parents who lived in Melbourne. This seemed a possibility, as we had both covered the journey by sea, and if you travelled by plane you didn't see much on the way except airport lounges.

Reading a Sunday paper one weekend, Graham, my husband, spotted an advert for Albert, the Australian bus. It wasn't actually Australian, but a London bus adopted by an Aussie couple! An immediate phone call told us that this bus was converted to sleep eighteen travellers, along with the owners; cooking chores were shared and prices for the trip established. Would we like to go and meet the couple and Albert?

We went the next weekend. It seemed like fun. But what if we didn't like some of the group? What if they were all single and we were the only married couple? Sleeping accommodation was only curtained off! What if we were sick and didn't want to travel on the next day? On the other hand, it would be the trip of a lifetime, visiting countries in Asia as well as Europe. If we had mechanical difficulties it wouldn't be our problem. We would be looked after, and most of the responsibility would be taken from us. But was that what we wanted? Decisions, decisions!

We decided it wasn't for us. If we were going to drive, then Graham and I would be the drivers. If we wanted to spend several days lazing by the Black Sea in Turkey, that would be our choice. We both wanted to feel the sense of achievement that we had accomplished this by our own efforts, even allowing for the difficulties we knew we would be bound to encounter. We did have a few problems, but we also met people who made the experience memorable by helping us overcome them.

So, we had made the first decision of many – we would buy our own vehicle and it would be just the two of us. That didn't mean we were not going to speak to as many experts as we could, read as much as we could and generally get as much help as possible in England before we left.

I can't remember how our neighbour, Mr Brown, initially knew about our plans but his was the sort of help we needed. A van with just two front seats and lots of space in the back seemed a sensible choice of vehicle. Our thoughts of a Morris minivan were dispelled by Mr Brown, whose advice was to go for a 'low-compression engine' (whatever that was!) and also a vehicle with higher ground clearance than a mini (I understood that bit!). We later met a couple who were indeed travelling in a minivan and we were pleased that we weren't!

Luck was on our side. Graham phoned me at school one day to say he had spotted a second-hand Morris 1000cc van for sale (a new vehicle was not even a vague thought). The Morris 1000 model was affectionately known as a 'moggie'. It turned out that our friend Mr Brown knew the owner and would speak to him on our behalf. Our first major expense – the vehicle bought for £465.

Mr Brown had spent many years in the pits at Brands Hatch and his mechanical advice and practical assistance before our departure set us up for success. His expertise was endorsed by British Leyland UK Ltd/Austin Morris group as it was known then. We contacted the motor company, who sent us details of their distributors throughout Europe; this was in a pre-printed booklet – obviously asked for regularly. They also enclosed another list typed especially for us, which included countries outside Europe and a final sentence saying they that regretted there were no contacts in Bulgaria or Afghanistan!

'OK,' said Mr Brown, 'I will draw up a list of spare parts you must take.' We were relieved that his list pretty much agreed with the list from BP/Shell fuel companies, to whom we had also written asking for advice. However, such phrases as 'No problems should be encountered in Western Europe' (did this mean problems were very likely in Eastern Europe or beyond?), and 'You'd better take an exhaust extension for crossing flooded rivers' did send an adrenaline rush through us for a few moments. Another source of help that was invaluable was the AA. Pre-printed routes, this time as far as Tehran in Iran (not just Western Europe), were readily available. Perhaps this independent travelling was getting popular. It was the route from Afghanistan onwards that had to be specially prepared. The AA was also able to help with documents, both for us and for the vehicle. Road maps for the later part of the journey were not easy to get, so these 'routes for your journey beyond Europe' were particularly important.

In those far-off days of the early seventies, the AA produced a voucher set which included a five-star travel certificate, a sort of travel insurance. More importantly for our peace of mind, it also included credit vouchers to the value of ninety-nine pounds, which were exchangeable for car repairs, legal assistance or airline tickets (for one person), and emergency repatriation vouchers. But once again all this assistance would only help us while we were travelling through Europe. It was only a small expense this time – eight pounds fifty for all this insurance cover. I know Graham appreciated this, wanting to be ready for all eventualities.

More paperwork for the van was required in the form of a Carnet de Passage en Douane. Again, the AA arranged this document which meant we could take the vehicle into Europe. However, they were not able to help with the indemnity policy required by the Indian authorities. Basically this was a guarantee that our vehicle would be leaving India and would not be sold there. The Indian government had strict control over the importing of foreign vehicles and spare parts. Even in these early days of planning, we were making contact with other cultures; the Indian bank manager at our local branch of Barclays understood perfectly what was required! This, together with green card insurance (would you believe, only for Europe), came to fourteen pounds.

Our local bank was also able to help with traveller's cheques and local currency. We were advised to take a little cash for those countries where you were allowed to carry their money prior to entering the country, and then to cash in a traveller's cheque. This would mean finding a bank or bureau de change close to the border. We actually found that a man would usually appear from nowhere as soon as we stopped after a border crossing, offering to change money. Unbelievable as it might seem sitting reading this now, we did actually trust and use the occasional chap. Partly we made use of these offers because, please remember, finding a bank meant transactions were only possible during opening hours, and then there needed to be enough time left within those opening hours to complete the transaction. This was in the 1970s, when ATM cash points were a thing of the future and overseas guests were to be enjoyed, feted and chatted to for as long as possible!

How about some of the paperwork required for humans and not vehicles? Passports obviously were needed, but so were visas. The difficulty here was you sometimes needed the exit visa for a country before you were allowed the incoming one. We had visions of being stuck in no-man's-land between two countries. Some visas had to be applied for in person at the embassy in London and then they had to be collected some days later.

We thought we had cracked this system, only for there to be a military coup in Afghanistan just days before our departure date. This meant the visa was nullified and had to be reapplied for, in person! Graham took the passports back to the embassy. There, the official casually put a black felt tip pen through the word 'royal' making it read simply 'Issued by the (Royal) Afghan Embassy'. Problem solved. However, this coup made the international press and was read by our increasingly anxious parents. Their anxiety was heightened by a short article concerning the bodies of two foreign tourists found by the roadside in the same country. It wasn't so easy in those days to reassure concerned relatives with regular travel updates.

International driving licences were simply obtained, thanks again to the AA. But we also needed vaccination certificates – cholera, typhoid and paratyphoid were the diseases of concern at the time and we needed proof that we were safe from these. This was not a pleasant couple of weeks! However, these vaccinations did highlight for us the need for first-aid supplies. We took all the usual medicines for cuts and headaches, and triangular bandages for breakages. We packed salt tablets and water-purifying tablets, insect-repellent sprays as well as Paludrine prophylactic tablets in case we still got bitten by malaria-carrying mosquitoes. Our skins were a distinct shade of yellow on our triumphant arrival in Melbourne. We were also advised to take in abundance a liquid medicine called J Collis Brown – this was for the treatment of 'a slight loosening of the bowels' and also for bad coughs! I still find this dual purpose odd and slightly amusing, but can only assume that it's not wise to cough if you are suffering with the other problem. All these supplies were packed in a small, clearly labelled suitcase and stowed under the passenger seat for easy access.

Other storage was not as easily accessible. We wanted to take lots of food and other supplies with us – really interesting things like toothpaste and toilet paper – partly to save on cost but also because we were not sure of availability. We would also need different clothes for the boating part of the journey. The biggest need was storage for the ever-growing pile of spare parts which were being gathered together by Graham and Mr Brown. So we decided to make a false floor in the van, as high as the wheel arches, to take suitcases, boxes of food supplies, etc. and the spare parts. This wooden 'floor' could be lifted at intervals to replenish the racks of food and other items which lined the walls of the van, while still giving us room for the sleeping bags in-between.

As the pile of boxes grew in our London house, we were pleased we had chosen the larger vehicle rather than the minivan. Our weekly shopping trip to the supermarket had begun to include items we laughingly called 'trip meat'. There were tins of meat but also tinned fruit, evaporated milk and packets of instant potato mix. Our local health shop advised us to take dehydrated vegetables as well as sachets and sachets of dried fruit juice, rich in vitamin C. The fruit juice was not particularly palatable, but it did help to disguise the taste of water with added purification tablets. We packed these into approximate weekly supplies and they were stowed under the false floor.

Although the majority of our travel was to be by road, we obviously had to cross water somewhere to get to Australia. This meant making shipping reservations. Being cautious travellers, we did not want to leave England without booking ourselves and the van onto the only boat sailing from Madras, in Southern India, to Penang, in Malaysia. This was with the British India Steam Navigation Company Limited, the cargo division of the P&O shipping company, on the SS *Rajula*, a coal-burning ship which took six days to cross the Bay of Bengal. Surprisingly and slightly worryingly, we were allowed to book for passengers and vehicle but were only allowed to pay for the passengers' crossing; the van had to be paid for in Madras, in Indian currency. An onward booking was also made with the Blue Star Line on the SS *Centaur* to take us from Singapore to Perth in Western Australia. But it was the sailing from India which we saw as the deadline. If we made it that far, we would be OK; we could be towed the length of Malaysia and push the van, if necessary. We had allowed ourselves eight weeks from England to Southern India.

By this time most of our friends were aware of our impending departure. Some said, 'Wow! You lucky things!' Others said, 'What will you do with your house? You've only just bought it.' The house problem did have to be sorted. We had decided to let it for a year, so were now busy advertising and interviewing possible tenants. This went very smoothly and the chosen couple agreed to rent our home, furnished, until the following summer.

We were getting closer to D – departure – day. I acted as the mate as Graham drilled bolt holes into the roof of the van to securely attach the second spare wheel. We had painted the roof white, as dark green didn't seem the most suitable colour in high temperatures. A small roof rack, purloined from an elderly aunt, took up the remaining space, with spare tyres chained and padlocked. Graham made an insect screen to cover the radiator grill at the front of the van and a jerrycan holder was fitted to one of the back doors to increase our distance between refuelling stops, if necessary. The false floor was made from chipboard to fit between the wheel arches, measured carefully so the suitcases fitted between the uprights, and boxes of food, toiletries and spare parts took up every remaining centimetre of space.

A couple of weeks before departure, Mr Brown gave the vehicle a thorough service. As well as the engine and braking system being given high priority, mundane jobs were also carried out, such as fitting locking wheel nuts. All the hydraulic lines under the van were sleeved in rubber tubing. A sump guard was fitted. The thermostat was removed but an extra blade added to the radiator fan to increase the cooling capacity. I said earlier that we were fortunate to have this gentleman's assistance and he also took great pleasure in the part he played in our success. One item in the spare's department that we decided not to take was a battery. Those of you who remember the Morris 1000 will know that the crank handle could be used to start the engine if needed, not that we did! Likewise, you may remember that the windscreen was flat, so we took a sheet of Perspex to make an emergency screen. The appendix lists the spares in full, many of which we 'sold' while staying at the YWCA in Madras.

All that remained now was for the end of my school term to arrive and we were ready to go!

Europe

a RATHER BOOZY FAREWELL SENT US ON OUR WAY AT LAST. We left south-east London on a Saturday evening in late July. I had worked until the end of term the day before, leaving Graham to pack, unpack and repack the van, as he had finished work the previous week. We had planned to cross the channel early on a Sunday. As neither of us had any experience of driving on the right-hand side of the road, we reckoned there would be less traffic at that time of the week.

On a previous drive into the Kent countryside we had found a campsite at the village of St Nicholas, only a few miles from the Hoverlloyd port at Pegwell Bay, near Ramsgate. We travelled down the M2, arriving about eleven o'clock at night. There was nobody around to book us in or see us leave the next morning. Very short on sleep, we left the campsite at 5 a.m. for the 6.30 crossing to Calais. This was pre-Channel Tunnel. A long-standing friend had very kindly travelled from Yorkshire to wave us on our way. The rather rough crossing did nothing to still the excitement, nerves, fears, worries and other emotions that we were experiencing after the months (or was it years?) of saving money, poring over maps and buying supplies, not to mention the constant discussions. Finally, we were on our way across the world. We had reached France!

We had anticipated correctly; there was very little traffic on the early morning hovercraft and so we were through customs and had left the hoverport within an hour of waving goodbye in England. The roads on the Sunday morning were very quiet which gave Graham the opportunity to experience driving on the 'wrong' side of the road, slightly more difficult in a van with no rear-side windows. He had packed really carefully but, even so, visibility was not 100%.

Goodbye England

Before lunchtime we had passed the first of our supposed camping spots – the first black cross we had drawn on the map on the sitting room floor in our London house, which was already beginning to feel a long way away. Our first night's stop was actually in Belgium. We had already covered 235 miles. We made a note in the logbook that there had been a lot of rain so the ground was rather soggy, but the facilities were reasonable with some shady areas. The charge per night was eighty-five Belgian francs – about eighty pence in 1973.

This was the only night we slept in Belgium. We moved on through Luxembourg the next day and over the border into Germany. A drive of 240 miles saw us at a campsite at Zeltplatzausweis. There were no problems with the facilities or the reasonable cost of five Deutschmarks – about the same as in Belgium. We were changing currencies rapidly in these days long before the euro, and we were also getting used to driving on the other side of the road. Graham was being very careful when turning left at crossroads, while I had to concentrate very hard when circling the rare roundabout. We had not got lost yet. We had surely got this travelling sorted! Therefore, in Austria we decided to take the scenic route rather than the tunnel; that is, the Grossglockner mountain road with its twenty-six sharp bends and a gradient of twelve per cent lasting for nearly forty-eight kilometres.

Not the best gradient for a fully loaded 8cwt van.

Graham's note in the log merely said: 'The mountain proved very difficult'! We saw nothing except thick cloud on the way up the mountain. The cloud was made worse by the steam rising from the bonnet of the van as the water in the engine boiled. We were not able to stop to cool down as the road was too narrow and we couldn't see if there were any vehicles behind – the suction rear-view mirror had fallen off with the cold. Our teeth were chattering by this time as we were dressed in shorts and T-shirts, with bare feet. The temperature hadn't just dropped a little, it had plummeted!

When we reached a stopping place at the summit, we still couldn't see more than a metre in front of us because of the blizzard. So much for the scenic route! That would teach us to be complacent. We didn't cover as much distance that day. However, we had learned a valuable lesson: we must treat our van with the greatest respect, we were going to be very dependent on it for the next eight weeks.

So, the next day we detoured to avoid even steeper hills with twenty per cent gradients and arrived in Yugoslavia. We decided that this day's drive was the most beautiful yet. We had a surprise lunch in a small restaurant near the border. Our limited knowledge of the Serbo-Croat language meant we thought we'd ordered fish and salad but we were soon eating lamb cutlets and potatoes! Don't be fooled – the sign for 'food served here' is a fish and a bottle. However, we did manage the bottle – local red wine – and very good it was too. This meal was much appreciated as it was the first we had not prepared for ourselves since leaving England. Had it only been five days ago?

Accommodation costs (campsites up to now) were still approximately eighty pence per night for both of us, sometimes including showers and separate cooking/eating areas, which meant we could preserve our own cooking gas canisters. We spent three nights at sites in Yugoslavia, including one only five kilometres from Belgrade. Another overnight stop was just through the city of Nis where the site was set out in numbered bays. The number we were allocated didn't match the bay we were directed to – due to our lack of Serbo-Croat again, perhaps. Otherwise, the facilities here were good, except for the toilet block – say no more.

Our limited knowledge of other languages was superseded by our complete ignorance of the Cyrillic alphabet, but we mastered the basic number system quickly after filling the petrol tank up one morning. We were learning to top up the petrol whenever we had the opportunity so we never needed more than twenty litres. The gentleman serving us demanded 300 dinars – enough for 100 litres. That would have been enough for a fleet of Morris vans! We handed him a wodge of notes to the approximate value of the fuel and drove away as he waved and shouted insults/abuse (who knows?) after us. This beautiful region of Europe has suffered civil war since our visit; hopefully the partitioning of Serbia, Croatia, etc. into states will now mean that peace is restored and visitors are returning.

We were back on track for our required distance covered each day since crossing the Alps. The landscape was changing. There were more farm vehicles, stockpiles of dried sweetcorn cobs and, of course, fewer tourists. Unfortunately, fewer visitors to the area meant that one petrol-pump attendant was not used to seeing locking petrol caps and, in his enthusiasm to serve us, completely vandalised the locking mechanism. This was to prove eventful later on when I stood up to a large Afghani gentleman.

Our first slow border crossing was experienced between Yugoslavia and Bulgaria, but it was just a slow process; no need to bribe the guards just yet, these weren't even touting guns, loaded or otherwise. Little did we know what lay ahead.

One night in Khaskovo – a campsite with very good facilities – cost only the equivalent of forty-five pence. Well, it was eight days after leaving the United Kingdom and we were about to cross into Turkey. As predicted by the AA, we had experienced no problems with our vehicle in Western Europe or indeed in Eastern Europe. The van had been driven on the 'wrong' side of the road in seven European countries but we were aware that perhaps the real adventure started here, as we crossed from Europe into Asia.

Turkey

THE BORDER CROSSING WAS AGAIN SLOW AND WE WERE amused at the string of young boys all along the main road between Edirne and Istanbul miming puffing cigarettes and calling after us. BP ran the campsite just twelve kilometres before Istanbul; our logbook record reads: 'wonderful with all mod cons'. It was a little expensive compared to what we had been paying, but we considered it good value with the facilities on offer and the welcome shaded areas. There was also a campsite run by the Shell petrol company just 500 metres down the road.

We stayed at this BP Mocamp for two nights because, for the first time since leaving home, we were hoping to collect mail. Remember this was before the internet café/email era. We had arranged poste restante at major post offices en route and we were looking forward to having letters from our families. Rather than drive into the city of Istanbul, we thought we'd try the local bus service. The dolmus was a minibus. It was cheap, crowded and would certainly not have passed a British MOT. However, the service was frequent. The disturbing aspect was that it did not actually come to a halt for passengers to get on and off – they were expected to run alongside for a few steps and then launch themselves through the open doorway into a vehicle that seemed bursting to the seams with passengers already. We managed!

A hectic day was spent on foot around the tourist sites of the city, and it was a welcome change from driving. Most impressive, we thought, were the Blue Mosque and the Sunken Palace, which was a metre under water. We were fascinated by the sites and sounds as well as the smells of the markets and bazaars. We had got off the dolmus at the terminus, in the heart of old Stamboul, and walked across the Golden Horn over the Galata Bridge.

When Istanbul was known as Constantinople, this was the only bridge. Later, after Turkey had become a republic, a second bridge called the Ataturk Bridge was built to cross the stretch of water, and this was the one we used to find our way back to the dolmus terminus.

We did indeed collect mail from the GPO and posted letters to our parents telling them that we were well and safe and happy. How much easier today's travellers must find keeping in touch with home – a quick text message on the mobile phone, always fully charged from the car's electrics. We had no regrets about the venture, although we were aware that the journey so far had been easy. We had not met any real difficulties and certainly no problems with the locals.

We left Europe proper the next day, when we crossed the Bosphorus, in those days done by ferry. We stopped for lunch at a *lokanta*, which consisted of *sis* kebabs with bread, salad and beer. Despite the heavy thunderstorms as we neared Ankara, we travelled 272 miles that day. I was surprised then that Graham still had some energy to waste attacking dozens of rats with our 'toilet' spade. The rats seemed to think our tent had been erected especially to shelter them. Graham's useless chasing at least gave the camp's nightwatchman plenty to laugh about. We slept in the van that night! Despite the company, this site, again supported by British Petroleum, had good cooking facilities and only cost thirty Turkish lire – less than one pound.

We were on the move early the next morning, checking out Ataturk's Mausoleum. The modern design and the setting in a large park area contrasted with the Citadel, which was dated 4500 BC, and sat on the top of a hill in the old part of the city. Ankara was a much quieter place than Istanbul, but it was here that we first saw armed soldiers, on duty at the entrance to the banks, brandishing automatic weapons as customers approached the doorway.

One similarity between Istanbul and Ankara, for travellers anyway, was that there were no signposts. Our small compass mounted on the dashboard saved the day, the first of several occasions on which it did.

We didn't drive down here, but left a young lad in charge of the van for a small tip.

Turkey struck both of us as a much more colourful country than Bulgaria; it had many adverts and roadside hoardings in bright colours. The fields we drove past had rice growing and we noticed farmers threshing the wheat crop by hand, with the help of a couple of donkeys. As we drove further east, the houses changed from the two-storey dwellings, with space for the animals underneath, to single-storey homes made from sundried mud bricks, where the animals shared the family accommodation. Goats, bullocks and water buffalo became commonplace, alongside the cows, sheep and donkeys. In the cities, young boys were selling water from large containers, while adult porters were bent double under loads resting on a type of saddle fixed to their backs.

Perhaps we left Ankara too late in the day, but when it got near dusk we were nowhere near a town, let alone a campsite. That night was spent on the open road, at a petrol garage, the proprietor of which spoke no English but did have a big smile. We got the impression, with the help of a packet of Benson and Hedges cigarettes, that it was fine for us to stay. There was no charge. Neither were there any 'facilities'. I shall not dwell on this, except to say the spade was not used for catching rats that night. Unfortunately, we didn't sleep too well as a large, noisy truck delivered fuel in the middle of a pitch-black night, and the attendant set fire to a couple of old tyres to see well enough to open the storage tank lids! We didn't get back to sleep after this.

An early start was the norm, but we were well on our way and swimming in the Black Sea by 9 a.m. What a contrast this area of lush vegetation was to the barren region of the Anatolian Plateau we had driven across near Corum. We spent a lazy day near Sampsun, swimming and sleeping, eating and drinking and giving ourselves a well-earned break. This was an idyllic campsite on the black, sandy beach under the pine trees, and it cost ten Turkish lire – equivalent to thirty pence in English currency. This Black Sea coastline was not really on the tourist map back in 1970s; today's travellers will find it very different.

Refreshed after our day's rest, we followed the coast the next day through Ordu and Giresun to Trabzon. This route gave us fantastic views. From Trabzon we turned inland and the road surfaces deteriorated. The rest of the day was on rough roads, these roads are referred to as 'stabilised' in the guide books and are 'best avoided'. We realised why when an emergency stop prevented us from a nosedive into a hole where the road was no more; a couple of locals had waved to us as we approached the chasm, but we were used to this acknowledgement of our important presence by now and simply smiled and waved back!

We were climbing all the time now and had reached an altitude of over six and a half thousand feet. Looking for a campsite, to no avail, brought us to the town of Bayburt. We had to pay forty Turkish lire for our accommodation – a room in the Sevil Palas hotel – but it did have a bathroom and WC. I got rather worried when Graham was supposedly collecting our overnight necessities from the van and hadn't returned to our room after forty-five minutes. When he did appear, it seemed he had been accosted by a local young man who needed help with his English homework.

Rather disconcertingly, the manager of the hotel felt it necessary to sleep in the hotel lounge to watch over our vehicle which was parked in the street outside the lounge window. Would you get that sort of service in an English hotel? This was indicative of the attention we received throughout this country; we were treated as guests, with the local people eager to make us welcome.

Having stated that we found the Turkish people very welcoming, we later met up with two lads in their late twenties who told us a different story. John and Paul were driving a Volkswagen Beetle in the same direction as we were, but we didn't catch up with them until India where they were shipping out of the same port. When in Turkey, they had an incident in a small town – a local elderly pedestrian was knocked down while John was driving. He then spent the next three weeks in a prison cell with about thirty Turkish prisoners, while Paul spent his days going between the British Embassy, trying to secure John's release, and the prison, where family members are responsible for the prisoners' needs – even their food. Although both chaps were putting on a brave face, I think it would take them a while to recover emotionally from this. There but for the grace of God go I!

It was the job of the non-driver to find Noah's Ark as we got closer to Mount Ararat; we crossed the Tahr Gecidi Pass at over 8,000 feet and saw the snow-peaked mountain, but not the boat.

As we drove up the main street of the town of Dogubayazit, the light was fading. We were on an unlit street with a very rough surface and a deep culvert right across it. Although we were not travelling fast (the previous night's hole saw to that), it made an almighty bang as the protective sump guard took the impact. We said a prayer of thanks for our friend back home, Mr Brown. A close inspection showed there was a deep crease in the metal, but it had served its purpose well!

That night was spent at a motel, the Motel Kent in Dogubayazit, at a cost of fifty lire. We had intended to camp in the motel grounds but decided to treat ourselves to a room, partly because of the tiring day's drive but really because of the washing facilities available to the campers! Little did we know what facilities were to be like later in the trip. We also treated ourselves to a meal at the local *lokanta* – kebabs and salad. The wine which accompanied the food was good and helped us forget the tour of the kitchen which the proprietor insisted upon. We agreed to the tour as the locals were being very friendly and we didn't want to mar international relations by being churlish, but if possible I would have given the tour a miss. In fact, if worried about cholesterol I would give the meal a miss or just have had the salad – no, perhaps not even that! This evening meal cost us twenty-four Turkish lire.

The road between Dogubayazit and the Iranian border gives some idea of the barren countryside.

However, the entertainment had not finished for the night. Our room was on the first floor in the motel, overlooking the hotel car park and the main road. We had a small balcony, a washbasin and twin beds. Graham awoke at 1 a.m. to a noise in the car park; he charged (starkers) onto the balcony to see a man on the roof of our van. After loud shouts and a Tarzan-like yell in readiness for jumping from the balcony, the 'car thief' informed us he was the hotel manager and was checking all the vehicles (all two of them) for security, and he was worried about the spare wheel on the van roof. Because we had a disturbed night we had longer to look for Noah's Ark, as our room overlooked the mountain, but we still couldn't find it.

Iran

THE TOWN OF DOGUBAYAZIT WAS ONLY THIRTY-FIVE kilometres from Iran so we detoured a little to see the ruined Palace of Ishak Pasha in the nearby hills before driving on to the Turkish/Iranian border. There were very few vehicles waiting to cross and we exited Turkey quickly. Entering Iran, however, was a lengthy procedure, with the Carnet de Passage for the van being required for the first time. It was also necessary to take out extra insurance in the form of third-party cover for our vehicle. It was worth it, as we were back on a bitumen road straight away. Our impressions of this new country were very positive as we approached the first town, Maku. There were houses with flower beds around, trees bordering the road, flags flying, and we saw our first camels. The terrain here was definitely greener than Turkey, but the children were very similar in finding us a source of interest.

Indeed, that night, travellers in our camping area felt very much as animals in a zoo must feel; we were the animals in the enclosure. We had travelled through Marand to the city of Tabriz and were directed by the police to the tourist compound in the south-eastern part of the city. We managed to squeeze the van into a tiny space between other vehicles inside the metal-fenced, gated and locked 'cage'. The perimeter of the compound was surrounded by families, because it appeared to be in a park area where the locals were taking an evening stroll. For the pleasure of being stared at until it was really dark, we paid fifty rials – about thirty pence. This was the first of nine nights that we slept in Iran and it was in this country that we began to encounter some difficulties, not with the people but with our health.

We moved on through Iran the next morning, travelling through towns with unfamiliar names: Bostanabad, Mianeh and Takestan. Our accommodation for the next night was at a hotel in the sprawling town of Qazvin. We took a walk up the main street during the evening. Most of the shops seemed to be either tailors or auto shops where you could see the work of both taking place.

29

We were accosted several times by beggars but were not unduly concerned for our safety.

The cost for one night at the Rahmani Hotel was 240 rials. The room had two beds which we named Colditz beds: wooden planks placed crossways for strength and a forty-five degree raised board at the head end to form a pillow (of sorts). They were about two-and-a-half feet wide but only five-and-a-half feet long, and had no mattresses, pillows or covers. Needless to say, we felt sleeping bags essential for some kind of comfort. I would point out that this was the more expensive of the rooms available, perhaps because it had a sink in it!

We may have given the bedroom only three out of ten, but we were happy to award the nightwatchman ten points for vigilance. He lived in a hut in the car park at the rear of the hotel. When Graham went out to the van later in the evening to bring in our cooking stove and food for dinner, he was challenged by the watchman. The Benson and Hedges cigarettes we gave him the next morning were most appreciated and it seemed a cheap price to pay for a good night's sleep!

The next day's drive brought us to the capital of Iran, Tehran. We had stopped and made camp by midday, at a campsite called Gol-e-Sahra; not just a well-shaded campsite with a shop, but the facilities also included a swimming pool. However, we couldn't relax in it just yet as Graham decided it was time for a pretty good look at the van. We carried out an oil change, checked the brakes, etc. and also did a fairly minor job consisting of tightening and refitting all the screws from the window and door panels that had fallen out over the bumpy Turkish roads. Talking to travellers coming from the opposite direction, we learned that the roads for the rest of Iran and also Afghanistan had good surfaces, but nevertheless we kept the screwdriver handy. Then it was time for that swimming pool!

As in Istanbul, we decided to use public transport to get ourselves to the centre of Tehran, particularly to the post office to collect mail from home. Again, this was a minibus and we boarded at just after 7 a.m. the next morning, travelling to Gomruk Square in the centre of the city. We also felt it vital to visit the Afghan Embassy to check the validity of our visas. The local taxi driver eventually found the building, where we were assured our visas were fine and that we had all the necessary documentation to cross the border in a few days' time. While in embassy mode we also decided to check the health requirements for the Caspian coast area, so we taxied to the British Embassy who confirmed we were unlikely to catch malaria from mosquitoes or cholera from infected water if swimming in the Caspian Sea. Then our minds were at rest to be proper tourists, so we took ourselves to the Gulestan Palace which was set in very pleasant gardens. City Park was equally pretty with flowers and fountains, giving a welcome impression of coolness. However, we were pleased to cool off properly in the swimming pool back at the campsite for the rest of the day.

We recognised several landmarks, especially Shahyazd Square, when we tackled the city centre of Tehran at 6 a.m. the next day. This venture was in the early 1970s, but by 1977 the Iranian people were destroying pictures and monuments of Shah Reza throughout Iran. Here we were taking photos of monuments bearing his name or statues showing his figure on horseback! It was only two years later that the Shah fled to Egypt. I don't think we would have felt at ease acknowledging that we were British if we had been travelling after Ayatollah Khomeini had begun to have so much influence over the Iranian people.

We approached the Elburz Mountains with some trepidation, (the Alps experience is imprinted in our memories till death), and although the surroundings were very barren, the road was not as bad as we had been led to believe by tourists travelling the opposite way to us. The road may have been better than we had anticipated, but the drivers here were very similar to the Turkish ones. We had read back home in our copy of the Fodor's guide that Turkey had one of the highest accident rates in proportion to the number of cars. Scary!

The towns of Rudehan and Polur took us to a height of nearly 7,000 feet. There were lots of tunnels through the mountains, the longest of which was about three kilometres. As we approached the Caspian Sea, the area became very fertile and green; there were lots of hotels, motels, picnic places and what we thought were holiday homes, looking rather Western in design apart from the aluminium roofs. This was probably the most prosperous area we had driven through since leaving Western Europe. The whole place seemed to be a retreat for wealthy Iranians.

This area was indeed in striking contrast to the rest of Iran. We had previously got the impression that small villages were abandoned when the houses deteriorated, or the grazing was all eaten or something, as we had seen many tumbledown houses along the roadside. Some of the buildings had flat roofs, others were dome-shaped. The small villages often had a wall around them. Before the Caspian Sea area, we had got used to seeing people (mostly men) asleep in the streets, possibly on a bed or frequently just using their shoes as a pillow and lying on the 'pavement'. The women also caught our attention as they were unfamiliar figures to us, dressed in dark clothes, usually with a shawl in a dark print design covering part of their faces.

Although we were so obviously a long way from home, there was the ever-familiar Coca-Cola for sale in even the smallest township; sometimes this was taken from a fridge, sometimes the ice covering it was simply brushed off, or on occasions the chipped bottles were pulled from a deep pit outside the shop, on the shaded side of the building. The water we were filling up with daily had got rather unpalatable by this stage of our journey; we were using the purification tablets which may not have helped with the taste and even the dehydrated fruit juice did little to conceal the flavour, so Coke had become quite a staple part of our diet.

One of many bread shops in Tehran.
One that has just come out of the oven, please!

As well as buying Coke from local shops, we were also buying bread – large, oval or round, thin and cheap. We usually tried to get a 'loaf' which we saw being taken from the oven so that it had not sat around on the counter as a resting place for flies.

Unfortunately camping did not seem to be a pastime of the rich and we had to pay for a hotel in the town of Behshahr at the high price of about sixty pence. For this we had a comfortable room. Pity then that we didn't discover till bedtime that not only could we not lock the door, we couldn't even shut it! It had to be barricaded with all the furniture that was mobile. Perhaps the 'open' door was to give us some fresh air, because when we drew back the blind to open the window, we discovered it was not an opening to the night air outside, but looked into the adjoining room!

As per usual, it was still early morning when we were ready for the day. A glance at the logbook told us we were averaging over 200 miles per day, so we would have been quite happy to relax on the beach at Bandashar, but it was not much good for swimming so we moved on. From paying 330 rials for a hotel room with no window and a door that didn't shut, we then paid fifty rials to sleep in the backyard of a hotel in Bojnurd on our way to the holy city of Mashad where we had our first bout of sickness.

As a centre of pilgrimage for Shi'ite Muslims worldwide, Mashad had a variety of accommodation for travellers, and we were given information about the campsite by the Iranian National Tourist Organisation. The site was spacious, although there was little shade, with rows of erected tents available for hire, but we still chose to sleep inside our vehicle. The facilities were limited and inadequate for the number of campers, but there was building work going on, which suggested improvements were being made.

The following day, we drove into the city to sightsee. The magnificent shrine of Imam Reza radiated out from the centre to the surrounding streets. Although non-Muslims, we were welcome to visit the shrine, and we also checked out the museum and Shah Square. We parked our van in one of the streets overlooked by the shrine and felt it was quite safe to do so. Another check of visas at the Afghan Embassy and another visit to the post office, and we then treated ourselves to a lunch of local food at an apparently hygienic restaurant. I say 'apparently' because that night I was very poorly! In our logbook all Graham wrote was 'bad night'. Some sixth sense told him to follow me after a few minutes across to the washroom block, where I was completely unconscious on the floor next to the non-Western toilet. We wore a track across the grass that night between our van and the toilet block. Whether it was the local food which my body took a dislike to, or a bug picked up in the water supply, we were not sure, but Graham was also suffering by the next day. We spent the time lying under the small amount of shade afforded by the few trees on the far side of the site. Did we feel miserable! By late afternoon Graham managed to find enough strength to walk to the local shop, as we both craved a dry biscuit. He returned with a packet of baby rusks which was the best he could do.

On one of his wanders to the washroom Graham spoke to an American gentleman called Wendle. A few minutes later he walked by our van with his wife Lucy and a thermometer. We didn't have one in our first-aid kit, as you know when you have a temperature. Lucy insisted on playing nurse and made the diagnosis that we both had the local bug which affects most, if not all travellers and usually lasts forty-eight hours. Whether it was this 'consultation' or the passage of time, by the evening we both were beginning to feel better.

The most important point which surfaced during the chat with this American couple was that we were rather dehydrated; we were not drinking until we felt thirsty by which time, in these temperatures, it was too late – you were already suffering. So we immediately took their advice and ignored the taste of the water, taking cups little and often from then on.

These new friends we had made were intending to drive through Afghanistan and then towards Bhutan and China. They were experienced travellers, older than us, and doing their driving in style in a spacious, air-conditioned motorhome. However, we were able to return their friendship when they came to check on our welfare the next day. They asked if we would mind them driving in convoy with us through the border crossing. 'Not at all,' we replied. So we left Mashad and proceeded to the Afghan border via Fariman and Turbat Jan, to the Iranian customs and police check. It didn't take more than half an hour to complete these formalities and we then passed to the incoming border control. The coolness of the American's motorhome was very welcome as the hours dragged on, as was the absolutely delicious scrambled eggs on toast Lucy rustled up to wile away the next hour. There were no other vehicles or pedestrians waiting to cross this border I might add, just us, completely subject to the whims of the border guards, police and doctor. Everybody, and I mean everybody, wanted a bribe. It was particularly difficult when the van was being checked. One lad, who looked about twelve years old but had a loaded rifle, wanted my camera; a larger, older-looking official wanted Graham's radio. However, after a lot of remonstrating, the custom papers were signed in exchange for two hundred cigarettes.

However, that was only the customs check, we still had the police check and the medical one to get through. After three and a half hours in ninety-degree temperatures the doctor OK'd our medical certificates and we were on our way to the town of Herat in Afghanistan.

Afghanistan

*B*ACK IN THE 1970S WHEN THIS TRIP WAS BEING PLANNED, I'm sure that a large proportion of the British population would have been unable to tell you that the capital city of Afghanistan was Kabul, let alone name any other of the cities in that far-distant country. Today, I personally know families whose sons are serving a term with the British forces as members of the peacekeeping units in the cities and remoter areas of Afghanistan. I mentioned earlier that there had been a change of rules in Afghanistan very close to our departure time. Indeed, the struggles there have a long history, and the more recent wars and economic upheavals are nothing new to this ancient country. The minor problem we had involving our visas was due to the fact that in 1973 the Afghan Communist Party and its leader, Daoud Khan, overthrew the ruling Afghan government's long-time king, Mohammad Zahir Shah. The monarchy was done away with and economic and social reforms instituted. Later, this government fell in another coup and the guerrilla, Mujahedeen, movement began. From not knowing the name of the capital city of this country, I would guess that ninety-nine per cent of British adults today know that Osama Bin Laden was offered refuge in Afghanistan following the Twin Towers atrocities in 2001. Is this a place I would wish my family to even step foot in, let alone drive through from the west via the south to the east? I think not! Yet here we were, travelling towards Herat.

The Park Hotel was a welcome sight. It took us a while to travel from the border as our American friends were having some problems with their super vehicle overheating, so we had to stop several times to cool down; we were sticking together after the border crossing problems. The next day Graham actually removed the thermostat from their Bedford. We could camp under the trees in the hotel grounds and we did for the second night of our stay. But, for this arrival night, we treated ourselves to a room as we were feeling shattered. It was really the fan in the room that sealed the decision. We would probably have paid more than the room rate of 100 Afghanis for this luxury (seventy pence well spent).

We spent a lazy morning under the fan in the hotel room, but stirred ourselves to explore the town later and it was delightful. The locals made us very welcome without being as forceful as the Iranians. It took a while to buy a couple of postcards as this meant a cup of tea and a long chat with the proprietor. We found a shop selling European foods and bought some tinned cheese, biscuits and cake. They were rather expensive, but we thought we deserved it. Herat felt a bit like an oasis in the middle of utter desert; it was the first sign of any habitation after crossing the border apart from camels and tent dwellings.

The trees provided welcome shade for several other campers beside ourselves.

The shops had wide open doors, presumably for coolness, but there were no goods on view outside. It was here we found our Coca-Cola kept in large stone pots covered with water, sometimes under the floor. In the streets we saw lorries and buses always decorated very colourfully, with lots of lights and platforms on the roofs crowded with passengers. There were carts pulled by horses brightened up with lots of red ribbons and bows. Out on the street also seemed to be the place to sleep, not as in Turkey where the locals might take a siesta, but beds were along the side of the road where adults and children settled down for the night.

We chatted to a family travelling the opposite way to us, a couple with a two-year-old daughter who seemed to take this journeying as the norm, and they told us of an hotel about 125 miles en route the next day which had a swimming pool. This sounded an easier way of keeping cool than our own version of air conditioning, which was wet towels hung up at the open windows as we drove along. This did work but, apart from actually drying very rapidly, it does not help the driver's visibility. Although there wasn't much traffic and very straight, concrete sectioned roads, it is perhaps not to be recommended.

So, spurred on by the thoughts of the pool, we made an early start. There was no difficulty identifying our target, as it was the only building for miles, and was called the Farrahrud Hotel. We were very welcome to make use of their green-watered pool. Indeed, there were others in the water. It wasn't until I had changed into my two-piece swimsuit and was about to jump into the coolish water that I realised there was not another female in sight. The occupants of the pool were all Afghan men with their young sons. There was not even an Afghani mum on the poolside. I expect the nationals were not impressed with a rather pale-skinned female in a bikini in their midst, but true to their position as hosts of their country, they smiled and nodded in friendship. Looking back now (it's easy to be wise with hindsight and all that), I realise that our actions did not show respect for the culture of the country we were visiting, and I hope that I would not make such a mistake again. But I'm not sure that if any woman did offend the locals today that they would get smiles in return.

The little boys soon grew tired and Graham and I then had the pool to ourselves. We spent a couple of hours in the water, knowing what the heat and humidity would be like as soon as we got out. Eventually we had lunch in the hotel: bread, rice and tiny bowls with meat and potatoes, which cost twenty Afghanis each – less than fifteen pence. Both of us wanted to delay driving on, so we chose to sample their tea, a strange blend of Indian and Chinese, which we found very refreshing. Unfortunately the effect doesn't last long in the high temperatures, but the heat had actually lessened by late afternoon when we made ourselves move on.

The town of Dilaram had a hotel and we stopped there in the early evening, setting up the cooking stove at the front of the hotel on the roadside. Whether it was the aroma of our tinned burgers and beans that attracted a small group of young men I'm not sure, but for the first time really since leaving home Graham felt uneasy. So we continued the smiles and nods, taking a photo of our inquisitive friends, but washed up quickly and packed away the cooking pots, then decided to hit the road. By this time the sun was very low in the sky so we had little choice but to drive in the dark, as Graham insisted that we put some distance between ourselves and the inquisitive young men.

We weren't worried about finding our way along this concrete road – built with Russian assistance, marked with posts every five kilometres starting at the Russian frontier at zero and ending just before Kandahar after 678 km – but we knew we had to be aware of booths at the roadsides where you were required to pay the next toll.

This 150-mile stretch doesn't look as forbidding in the daylight.

From our AA route planner, we knew where these tolls should be and sometimes where the counterfoil was to be collected, often a hundred miles or so further on. There were six in total in Afghanistan, not five as the planner had indicated. We didn't query whether the sixth was legitimate! The booths were sometimes just a hole in a small building set back from the road and at night lighting was minimal. At other points there were barriers across the road so you couldn't really continue. It was only a few days back that we had crossed the border with the loaded rifles on display!

It was 11.30 p.m. when we pulled into the rear of the Greens Hotel in Kandahar after five hours' driving across, as Graham put it, no-man's-land. Officially, our route had stated scrubland and desert. Our van's headlights on full beam shone straight into the rear window of a camper van at which two very startled faces suddenly appeared. We hastily switched off as we waved an apology. A formally worded apology would have to wait till daylight. We were too exhausted to do more than climb into our sleeping bags in the rear of the van, among the debris from supper time, all because Graham had had an uncanny feeling it would be wise to move on.

The next morning when we could see our surroundings we decided we must have chosen the worst hotel in the town, if there were any others. We were plagued constantly by the hotel manager for any items, but especially cigarettes. We paid him twenty Afghanis for the use of his cold tap, apologised to the two men in the camper van who had thought their number was up and drove to the town centre.

Talking to other overlanders, especially those travelling in the opposite direction, gave us bits of information about road conditions, places to stop or shop, as well as local customs. One conversation had been about the local flea markets. Although we had brought lots of spare parts with us, other travellers were not as cautious and had bought vital spare parts from a market stall. There was a joke passed round that you could have your spare wheel, wing mirror or number plate stolen from your vehicle one day, only to buy it back the next day in the market.

Well, we needed money and this meant a visit to a bank. We

knew it would be best not to leave the van unattended after all the stories we had heard and our own gut feelings as well, so we parked in the central square in the town and tossed a coin to decide that Graham would go into the bank while I played guard in the van. Remember, bank visits were very lengthy procedures. The counter clerk would usually call the manager, then you were escorted to another room, where a drink of refreshing but unsterilised water or tea would be offered. Passports were then scrutinised and several, if not all, bank staff were called in to also look through the documents. Phone calls were perhaps made there and then to check current exchange rates. Sometimes sign language was used to explain that a phone call needed to be made, but phones were out of action and it would take an hour or so.

That day's bank visit followed the usual pattern and I sat in the van expecting it to be at least an hour before Graham would reappear. I slumped in the passenger seat, trying to catch up on some sleep, but rousing every few minutes to look around at the hustle and bustle of Afghani town life. Suddenly, through the wing mirror, I saw a tall gentleman in the common blue robes of local dress standing at the back of the van, just gazing nonchalantly around. I looked but did not sit up higher in the seat; the said gentleman, I can only presume, did not realise I was in the van. As I watched, unable to believe my eyes, he put out a hand and untwisted the damaged locking petrol cap from its place and put his hand behind his back, still standing in the same spot. I did not even hesitate for a second but with the thought of local flea markets and stolen car parts buzzing around my head, flung open the van door and hurled out a stream of English accusations, abuse and nonsense at the man. He still had not moved. I've no idea what he was thinking but without saying a word he drew his hand from behind his back and handed me the petrol cap. Then he slowly walked away.

Only then did I begin to shake. I put the cap back in place and looked over at the bank entrance, but there was no sign of Graham, of course. I spent the next half hour standing by the van, walking round it but not sitting inside. Graham's first comment when he eventually reappeared was to ask why I was standing outside in the heat and not taking advantage of the shade!

We now had money and could pay the tolls that we expected on the drive between Kandahar and Kabul. The exchange rate, however, was not in our favour. Before leaving England we had checked all rates for foreign currency and in London we could buy Afghanis at 240 to the pound; that day, the best Graham could do was 150. Within two months the rate had dropped by over one third. Nevertheless, if you want to compare costs with today, it is interesting to note that for six nights' accommodation in Afghanistan, plus petrol, plus border insurance and road tolls we spent the grand total of twelve pounds and twenty pence. Not bad, even if the accommodation wasn't exactly five star.

We were now travelling on a concrete highway which had been built with American assistance. It was a gradual climb through more scrubland following the River Tarnack, although close to the water there was some cultivation with crops of wheat and sweetcorn. At the highest point we were at about 9,000 feet before descending slowly along a rather winding stretch. In a few places the road had collapsed as a result of heavy rain in the previous few months. After a couple more tolls/checkpoints we were approaching the suburbs of Kabul.

We met up with our American friends again, here, at the Ariana Hotel. This was *the* place for overlanders to 'camp'. It was a large hotel in its own walled grounds. We found a spot at the rear of the building, rather too close to a very large pile of rubbish. Any attempts Britain has made to recycle its waste over the last thirty years would be put to shame by the handful of youngsters who seemed to spend all daylight hours on this heap of rubbish. We paid twenty Afghanis per person, per night for the view! We didn't pay cash for all the three nights, however, as we bartered a tin of baked beans for one night's accommodation!

We were pleased to have a couple of lazy days and caught up on the mundane jobs of washing clothes and checking the van over. The infamous Khyber Pass was looming. The thought of a hot shower was a pleasant one after the last couple of days' travel and we headed up the imposing central staircase of the hotel in the direction of a bathroom. I have never had a shower as quickly as at the Ariana Hotel! It was also here I learned to take, and hold, very deep breaths. Even today, the stench that greeted me as I opened the shower-room door is conjured up when I think about it. I took a deep breath through my mouth, held it as long as possible and then exhaled very slowly, while at the same time soaping and rinsing under the trickle of warm water. Three breaths and I was out of there!

We walked into Kabul to collect mail from the post office via our poste restante arrangements. As before, this worked without any hitch and we were in touch with our families again. I don't know if this service is available today, or if the post office is still standing in Kabul. I may have been the only unveiled female around, but we walked the streets without any hesitation for our safety. The only sign that there had been a coup just weeks back was a night-time curfew for the locals in the capital, but otherwise we saw nothing to worry us back then.

Leaving Kabul early the next morning meant we said farewell to our American friends, who were heading for Kabul airport north of the city to stock up with supplies at a supermarket on the American airbase. They intended to travel on through Northern India en route to Bhutan, but were uncertain whether they would be allowed to proceed from there to China, hoping to later ship back to the States.

We proceeded towards the Afghan/Pakistan border via Jal-al-abad. We knew there were about one hundred and fifty miles to the Khyber Pass in West Pakistan, which was only open from dawn to dusk. Our final goodbyes to Afghanistan were at the town of Dakka, where the customs and police posts were located. We had nine miles of no-man's-land to travel across to the customs and police station at Torkham in Pakistan.

Pakistan

WE WERE RELIEVED TO ARRIVE AT THE PAKISTAN BORDER control and exit the nine miles of barren no-man's-land. This was a fenced area like a huge zoo enclosure and we were aware that we were locked in. For us to enter Pakistan the police had to unlock the large wire gates where friendly officials greeted us. Formalities were completed quickly, including the toll required to enter the Khyber Pass, which was four rupees for the van and one rupee per person. We were advised by the authorities that entry had been logged and our safe exit would also be recorded. Under no circumstances should we stop within the Pass due to frequent activity of bandits!

During its history, the Khyber Pass has been an important gateway from central Asia into the plains of the Indo/Pakistan subcontinent. Many conquerors have forced their way through its dangerous terrain for the riches further east. Starting from the foothills of the Suleman Range, it gradually rises to a height of three and a half thousand feet. As well as the road route we would use, a railway line, considered to be a great feat of engineering, also passes through. The road wound below the Jamrud Fort and under the Khyber Gate. It was with a great sense of achievement that we safely exited this famous Pass, after a difficult and dangerous climb through its series of hairpin bends, sheer drops and dark tunnels.

With the Khyber now behind us, we travelled the remaining nineteen miles into Peshewar, arriving mid-afternoon. There were signs of flooding on our approach to this region, with some road diversions in place but as we knew it was the very end of the monsoon season we were not unduly concerned. Little did we know what lay ahead!

Within the Pass – a rugged, sheer and isolated beauty.
No bandits around when we took this photo!

Although Pakistan is a Muslim country, the Deans Hotel, where we spent the night, allowed us, as European guests, to purchase two bottles of Tiger beer. This involved signing their alcohol register, but the refreshing result was worth all the paperwork. Imagine doing that for a beer in England! The cost to stay in their car park was twenty rupees – rather expensive at eighty pence. We were able to pay this in local currency with the assistance of a little man who appeared from nowhere and offered to cash a traveller's cheque for us. We had little choice but to trust this chap. We were quite happy with the exchange rate when he returned promptly, asking for only two rupees for his trouble.

After the dry, barren expanses of Afghanistan, the lush countryside of Northern Pakistan was a vivid contrast with greenery, fruit trees and even roses. However, the humidity was unpleasant enough to force us to lay our sleeping bags on the gravel car park; to sleep inside the van would have been impossible and pitching the tent in their garden did not seem to be the thing to do.

Although we were grateful to our financial agent, we had only trusted him with a small-denomination cheque, which meant we needed to visit the bank the following day. Again, as was common since leaving Turkey, the bank was well guarded by men carrying double-barrelled shotguns – they did look businesslike! The transaction only took one hour that day and then we were on the way to Rawalpindi. En route we crossed the Indus River using the combined road and rail Attock Bridge. We travelled along the Grand Trunk Road which was fairly wide and busy but we arrived safely in the city after our first full day in Pakistan.

The accommodation for this night was at the Gatmells Motel, in their shaded and furnished garden area. They also provided us with good bathroom facilities, which was a bonus after earlier experiences. We happily parted with six Pakistani rupees for our stay – approximately twenty-four pence – which was better value than the previous night's gravel. We would have appreciated a second night there, but felt we needed to keep to our planned schedule and it was a good job we did. Whether these good facilities had anything to do with Rawalpindi being a British garrison town in the mid-nineteenth century or being the capital of Pakistan after the partition in 1947 I don't know, but later Islamabad, which is positioned about ten miles north-east, became the capital. It was expected, even in the 1970s, that the two cities would eventually merge to become one very large metropolis.

Continuing along the Grand Trunk Road out of Rawalpindi, the damage from the monsoon flooding became more obvious and then troublesome. Was it any wonder there were problems after one hundred and sixty-eight inches of monsoon rain in the preceding four weeks? One bridge on this main highway had been destroyed and so we had to use a pontoon bridge to cross the River Chenab after queuing for an hour in the sweltering heat among a swarm of inquisitive people. As well as these temporary bridges, put in place by the army, there were also lots of aid tents supplying food, blankets and other essentials. And we were complaining about an hour's wait!

Road repairs were underway. This involved ladies at intervals along this important road seated next to a pile of large rocks. Each worker had a hammer which she was using to transform the large rocks into small pieces of gravel. Other workers made a continuous chain, carrying baskets of gravel to nearby areas requiring repair. Although it was only about one hundred and seventy miles to Lahore, it took us until late afternoon to reach the city, where we first collected mail from the post office, before finding the YWCA hostel and camping within their grounds at a cost of five rupees.

Everyone sleeps on these; we did likewise.

It was here we were given two beds by the gatekeeper, one of which was his, and slept comfortably under the stars. Well, one of us got a good night's sleep. Graham had forgotten the advice given earlier on the travels about watermelons. It had been emphasised that melons did not grow in the towns but were carried from miles away. Days later they were freshened up overnight in the open drain channels near the vendor's stall. To assist this they were first punctured with a skewer to enable the liquid to be easily absorbed – facelift completed! Graham had really enjoyed several chunks of the said melon a couple of hours earlier, but was violently sick during the night. Lesson learned this time.

Lahore is the capital of the Punjab region of what was then West Pakistan. This country is now simply known as Pakistan but was differentiated from East Pakistan, which we now know as Bangladesh. One of the most impressive buildings we visited in Lahore was the Badshahi Mosque, built of red sandstone and white marble. We also paid a visit to the local cinema, where the film fortunately had English subtitles as our Urdu was no better than our Serbo-Croat. The other lasting memory is the thousands of bicycles.

Although Graham was still feeling the after-effects of the watermelon fiasco, the next morning we left Lahore for the Pakistani border control at Wagah. At this time of world currency restrictions, the legal limit for export of Pakistani money was forty rupees. We had not committed this fact to our long-term memory and had considerably more. However, the police came to our rescue and offered to change the surplus into Indian currency. Never mind that importing Indian rupees was also illegal and punishable by a prison sentence! We accepted his exchange rate of 100 Pakistani rupees for eighty Indian rupees.

While our road permit was being scrutinised, we were being questioned as to where our children were, and why after three years of marriage we had none. They also asked which contraceptive had we used for it to be so effective! These questions were asked in a friendly manner and we hoped our answers were useful to them! Farewell to Pakistan.

India

*A*PART FROM THE IMMEDIATE EUROPEAN COUNTRIES, INDIA is the only country I have revisited, and intend to go to again. Nehru himself is reported to have said that 'the diversity of India is tremendous... It lies on the surface and anybody can see it'. One of the many books we read prior to leaving England was *Fodor's India.** On the first page it is written that the country offers something for everyone, and a little later that, 'It can be felt, sniffed and heard the moment the visitor first touches shore...' How true! Welcome to India.

The Indian customs and immigration at Attari were more formal and didn't ask as many personal questions. They wanted rather to see the detailed list of spare parts that were being imported into their country (in transit only). Our enquiries about car insurance were met with the reply that we did not need it! The van was searched and one suitcase opened. Our tourist guidebooks, which were found in the glovebox, were studied with interest and we were also asked how many rupees would we accept for our cameras! No cigarettes changed hands at this border crossing.

We may not have been asked questions about our family-planning methods by the customs officials, but both they and the border police did want to know about any troop movements we had seen. There seemed a lot of tension still between Pakistan and India and several questions were put to both of us as to where and how many soldiers we had seen. Our answers were all rather negative. I assumed this was a good thing.

The crossing we used was not the one on the AA's prepared route, but we were doing fine with finding our way in these

---

* Donald S Connery, 'Initiation to India', in Fodor's 1973 Guide to India, ed. by Eugene Fodor and William Curtis, Hodder and Stoughton, 1973, p.89

countries. We wanted to visit the city of Amritsar in Northern India to see the famous Golden Temple, but it would have to wait until the following day as Graham was still feeling rather poorly. This meant he stayed in the vehicle while I visited the tourist-information centre to find out about accommodation; our guide books were invaluable, but did not give us details on how to find the hotels mentioned.

Although we had crossed into a new country, the feeling of being welcome guests was apparent immediately. This meant a lengthy stay in the tourist office being refreshed with iced water before I was even asked the reason for being there. Practice makes you very good at sipping water without actually drinking any, although I could have done with a large plant nearby and a moment or two when I was paid a little less attention.

This led to a stay at an inexpensive Indian-style hotel called the Imperial. It may have only cost thirty Indian rupees (a little more than one pound fifty) for our double room, but it was really quite luxurious compared with some places we had used. It had very large rooms, with a dressing room in addition to the bedroom, as well as a bathroom; in all the rooms, the ceilings were about twenty-feet high, which made them fairly cool, but this was improved with a very large ceiling fan. We parked the van directly outside the French windows leading straight into our room. The other way in was via the central hallway of the hotel; as we stayed here for two nights, we used the French doors more often, in the hope that the hotel proprietor may not have seen us return. If he knew we were in, we were served tea immediately and at approximately half hourly intervals. However, it was very refreshing tea and, we thought, safer to drink than other liquids as the water would probably have boiled. The other refreshments, which we were offered in large quantities, were eggs – poached or boiled. We had seen the chickens roosting on the van roof the first evening.

The next morning saw us in a trishaw being pedalled to the Golden Temple, a central place of worship for the followers of the

We were welcomed at the Golden Temple.

Sikh religion. The city of Amritsar was founded by the fourth Sikh guru, and the name means 'pool of nectar'. The pool is surrounded by white marble with the temple itself being reached by a marble causeway. Although the sacred book of the Sikhs, the Granth Sahib, lies in the sanctuary, there were no restrictions on who could visit this place, although the removal of shoes was required. I do hope that this is still the case, although I wonder if the horrors of terrorism have had repercussions. Certainly in 1973, as Christian visitors to this impressive building, we were acknowledged as welcome guests and, as far as I could tell, we were the only non-Sikhs present.

Our trishaw pedaller was waiting for us, presumably antici- pating a return fare. He took us first to the bank and then returned us to the hotel, although on two occasions he asked us to get out and walk as the road was going uphill! To be fair, he was one of the more elderly drivers we saw. Unfortunately, he asked for an extortionate amount of money when we got out. This gave me time to take a photo of Graham arguing with him; looking back, I suppose he assumed we were wealthy tourists, and compared to him we would have been considered rich.

Later in the day, we walked to the post office in Amritsar to send a telegram. A family member back in England was getting married shortly and obviously we were going to miss this. I wonder, do people under the age of thirty know what a telegram is? We could have been forgiven for thinking the people of the Punjab did not understand them either as sending one was such a lengthy procedure. First, you had to get through the door of the post office building; second, you had to make your way between people, mostly men, to the counter; third, you had to ask for a form to send an overseas telegram... I could go on. Let's just say this afternoon was mostly spent inside the post office. However, the mission was accomplished at the cost of twelve rupees. How much easier today's youngsters would find it – just send an email for the best man at the wedding to print out and read at the reception! We treated ourselves to an ice cream from a street vendor on the way back to the hotel. When would we learn to follow advice on what not to eat in unfamiliar places? However, we got away with it this time. Possibly because it was followed almost immediately by more tea.

We left early the next morning and picked up the printed route at Ludhiana. This would lead us about two hundred miles to Delhi, along the Grand Trunk Road, a route that goes way back in India's history. Perhaps this is the time to mention road rules. Generally, the only speed limit was thirty miles per hour in the cities. The Highway Code doesn't mean a lot if you are in charge of a bullock cart, where time is not measured in minutes, or even hours. The bullock cart would be in the middle of the road and your horn would probably cause much confusion as one animal pulls to the nearside and the other to the right. Then there are the cyclists who assume they have the right of way over cars, lots of dogs, perhaps monkeys, and absolutely everything stops for the sacred cow asleep in the middle of the road.

The Grand Trunk Road.

The days' mileages were much lower than earlier on the journey, but it didn't matter as everything was so fascinating to look at. We didn't make it to Delhi in one day, but stayed the night at a rest house in Karnal – this one was provided by the National Dairy Research Institute. Generally, in small towns, there are government-owned establishments where tourists are welcomed, but really they are meant for travelling officials. These are categorised, with dak/traveller bungalows and rest houses being at the bottom of the ladder. The accommodation is limited – one or two rooms only. This one, as was common, did not even provide bedding. This area of India, Punjab and Haryana, had evidence of much dairy work, but we were still surprised to come across milk bars serving the public, run in one instance by UNICEF.

We only had eighty or so miles to travel the next morning and we were in Delhi by midday visiting the Red Fort, which was built in 1648 behind red sandstone walls from which it gets its name. It's easy to imagine an elephant carrying a Moghul prince in a silver *houdah* here. When you leave the Red Fort, you get into Old Delhi with its crowded bazaars and narrow, congested streets where life goes on in public, whether it be a shoemaker mending sandals or men being shaved with small sickles next to a cow chewing vegetables from a stall. A strange aroma fills the air; I think it's spices.

We camped that night at the scout camp near Humayum's Tomb, another of the glorious buildings in the same style as the more famous Taj Mahal. Perhaps scouts are hardier than us, but we found the facilities here more than primitive and the flies were especially troublesome. Still, what can you expect for three rupees? We were relieved to drive into New Delhi the next day. Such a contrast, with wide, tree-lined roads. We didn't really go for the bears with collar and lead being walked along the roadside, but we found the abundance of monkeys quite amusing. We had to do the touristy thing and drive along the Rajpath, the broadest avenue in Delhi where you can see government buildings as well as the presidential palace. Apparently, proceedings in the Rajya Sabha (Council of States) and Lok Sabha (House of the People) are in Hindi, as the national language, or in English. There are fourteen major languages as well as over two hundred dialects, but what else would you expect in a country whose population was second in number only to China and made up of many ethnic groups.

It is said that the visitor to India will fail himself if he sees only the Taj Mahal and the interior of his air-conditioned hotel. We hadn't seen many air-conditioned hotels on our journey, but we were keen to get to the Taj Mahal in Agra. A new type of accommodation awaited us there – a Methodist Mission guest house. We learnt during the evening that one missionary aim is to support education. This particular centre ran two schools, an English-speaking one costing fifteen rupees a month and a cheaper version at only five rupees which taught in Hindi. Although the mission provided schooling up to eighth class, most of the children stayed only until fifth class, before the start of what we would call secondary education.

We ate our evening meal, which was, fortunately, cooked for us before the thunderstorm caused the power supply to fail. We had heavy rain during the evening, all night and while we breakfasted. The rain had stopped but the sun was not shining when we visited the Taj. In our logbook we wrote that this building was the most impressive, even without the reflection, the highlight of any public building we had seen. I can see why the Taj has lured travellers to India for centuries.

In retrospect I think our trouble with the monsoon began in Agra that night. All our preliminary reading had told us that the monsoon crosses India during June and July and we were now in late August. While television communication today can bring us vivid pictures of the power of natural disasters, I think it is difficult to imagine the force of nature unless you experience it for yourself. We filled up with petrol and the rain began again as the attendant replaced the hose. We ran inside to pay and shelter for a few minutes, then walked back ankle-deep in water and realised the rain was not about to stop. We moved the van out of the way and sat; we could not possibly drive. Because we had spent the previous evening with English speakers, we had been discussing the local newspaper report on the road conditions. Our enquiries at the tourist office confirmed the article in the paper that the bridge on the Gwalior road was down and that the usual ferry on the same river crossing was not running because of heavy rain. However, we found a detour, followed by a detour from the detour as further enquiries about a second bridge forced us to drive three hundred miles instead of the expected one hundred and twenty. Eventually we crossed the offending river Chambal and it was after ten o'clock that night when we took a room in a hotel in the town of Jhansi, about which I can remember absolutely nothing!

So, were all our rain problems over? Lighter rain fell all the next day, but our windscreen wipers coped with it and there were no more detours. Several overturned trucks along the roadside did concern us a little; the roads were narrow with very soft edges. We were not going to argue if one of the large, decorated trucks, common in the area, came towards us, but we carefully made sure that we were far to the left but still on the tarmac if possible. There was just about room, but definitely not enough for two trucks to pass and this was very evident.

Through the rain, we were able to notice the change of vegetation as we travelled towards central India, which was more tropical with bananas in abundance. Camels and elephants were part of the daily life going on around us as we drove through small towns and villages. Women usually carried a variety of goods on their heads – water pots, enormous piles of grass/hay and sometimes sheets of corrugated iron. Children and adults were begging. We felt guilty as we shooed them away, but whenever we stopped within seconds there was always a group of children surrounding us, sometimes with goods to buy – 'lady's finger' bananas – but always with outstretched arms asking for baksheesh.* The houses too seemed to be different from the brick/mud buildings of the north. We were now seeing wooden shelters, often with interwoven branches and leafy roofs. Sheep, goats and cows were in and around the homes. We also noticed a change in the dress of the locals. Just as we saw the change of headgear from the Pakistani Muslims to the northern Indian Sikhs, we were told that white hats were worn by the followers of the congress party in central India. The women in their brightly coloured saris all looked elegant, no matter what work they were doing – despite the fact that, because of the monsoon rains, there was mud everywhere!

Our next night's accommodation was another first – one of the government-run rest houses. This was just outside the small town of Binaganj. It cost us thirteen rupees – a little expensive you might think for no running water, hot or cold! Believe me, we were very pleased with the facilities on offer for the charge – a large room with a bed, easy chairs, dining table, etc. as well as a smaller bedroom. There was also a bathroom with a plentiful supply of water in pots as well as a toilet, and the van was parked at the door! When I say 'toilet', I don't mean a 'Western-style' one, as they are sometimes called. The bathroom consisted of a large clay bowl, several large, full water pots, a concrete floor with a drain hole at one end and a larger toilet hole. There was a smaller clay pot to use as a flushing utensil. The bathroom was reached along a little, narrow passage from the main room. It was just as well we had such luxurious accommodation as Graham was not well during the night but had another dose of Delhi belly. We were fine, though, because we discovered the next morning

---

* 'Baksheesh' is a term used to describe tipping and charitable giving in the Middle East and South Asia.

that the adjoining room was taken by a female doctor visiting isolated villages in the area. This type of guest is why the rest houses are really provided.

Graham seemed to be fit enough to leave the bathroom and so we were ready to move on, if a little later than our usual time. That day proved to be a rather frustrating one, partly because of the continued bad weather, but also due to language difficulties and van trouble! It started off rather wet and windy as we drove to the small town of Baiora. Most of these towns seemed to have just one main street and this was no exception, but this single street had an unusual number of parked vehicles. The streets were lined with colourful lorries – we had become used to seeing these by now. These were the same type we had hoped not to meet on the narrow strips of bitumen on the roads. Invariably, they were loaded to bursting point with freight, passengers perched on top, and up to six people in the extended cab – not held in by any doors, of course. The weight and sheer number of these vehicles in Baiora had turned the street into a mudbath. I'm not sure what had happened to the tarmac. There were so many parked trucks that something must be wrong. Enquiries at the police station eventually told us that the road was blocked by floods and that two bridges, about eight miles apart, were submerged. We had been warned that asking for directions in India was not a good idea, because the Indian people are too polite to foreigners to say they don't know and we were beginning to see the truth in this. As the first of these submerged bridges was about ten miles up the road and our enquiries about how long before the road would be clear had told us absolutely nothing, we decided to take a look for ourselves.

Sure enough, the water was about ten feet over the bridge! One man was attempting to walk across, but had to turn around when the water reached his chest. Further enquiries, involving the familiar head shaking and nodding or both at the same time replies which we were beginning to interpret as yes and no or I really don't know, did not uncover a detour that was passable, so we returned to Baiora to get accommodation for the night at the rest house. According to our valued AA route there was one in the town, but of course it was full.

So, Plan B – back to the government rest house at Binaganj, only to find that our room was already reserved for the night. We did not want to retrace our steps further in the wrong direction and eventually managed to get a room at the lodge in Baiora. This was accommodation for truck drivers and you paid for a bed only; each room containing several beds, a light and nothing else. We managed to persuade the manager to remove one bed in one of the smaller rooms and we paid five rupees, instead of the usual arrangement of two rupees per bed. It was a noisy night! This small town was packed with people, mostly male; trucks were 'parked' in long lines along a 'highway' ankle-deep in mud; all along the roadside were huddles of men cooking their evening meals under leaden skies. There was much coming and going and general chat as all the rooms, and in fact every space where a body could lie down, were occupied.

As I've mentioned, van trouble had been a problem this day; some of the roads between these two towns were under repair and we thought the sharp chippings had caused our first puncture, but we weren't going anywhere. In fact, our tubeless tyre and the mechanic's attempts at repairing it was a welcome amusement to a small group of twenty or so drivers. Eventually the tyre was inflated, but not very successfully. It was later in Bangalore that a mechanic decided that the only solution was to put a tube in the tyre, as they did not have the air pressure to inflate a tubeless tyre satisfactorily.

I shall never forget the respect with which I was treated early the next morning when I knew I would have to visit the 'bathroom'. I could hear the conversations being carried on outside our room and peered through the wooden shutters to see long lines of men queuing to use the facilities – two non-Western toilets with doors. One of the dominant traits of the Indian character is hospitality. There was very little we could be offered in this situation and yet as soon as I walked hesitatingly to join this queue there were calls of 'memsahib' and gestures to the front of the line.*

Our enquiries to the truck drivers as to when the road might

---

* 'Memsahib' is the female equivalent of 'sahib' meaning 'sir', the respectful title used by Indians when addressing an English person.

be passable met with many different answers, ranging from three o'clock today to three days, so we decided to check with the police, whose words of wisdom consisted of simply 'proceed'. As we had nothing to lose, except maybe our beds, and nothing else to do, we loaded the van, fully expecting to unload it an hour later, and did proceed to the first bridge.

I shall never understand where all this water went during the night.

To our utter astonishment, the bridge was visible with the water flowing about five feet under. It had been slightly damaged and was covered in bits of debris, but we had no trouble crossing. We then came to a halt about two miles before the second bridge and joined a queue. We waited for about three hours and then everyone moved forward to cross the river Newaj. This bridge took a little careful negotiating as some of the cobbles had been washed away, but we didn't get the wheels in any gaps and were safely on our way. A mere hundred miles and no detours took us to the town of Indore. We had been told by a PWD (Public Works Department) driver back in Baiora that our troubles would not be over when we reached Indore, so the next morning began with a visit to Indore bus station for any information we could glean about the Narmada River. What we were told was that the river was in flood and was blocking the Agra/Bombay road about forty-five miles away. The water was said to be thirty-five feet above the bridge. No amount of asking at several petrol garages told us anything different! We were on our way back to the rest house when we stopped to ask yet again. This time we asked a gentleman wearing Western clothes and not the now-familiar dhotis; we thought, correctly, that he might speak enough English to be able to help us. What hospitality was shown! What a super day we had!

Firstly, we were invited into his house to look at a map and to find us an alternative route to Madras avoiding Bombay. It was now September and the July monsoons were causing such problems. However, we could not look at the map until we had drunk tea. This was accompanied by a homemade sweet rather like fudge and some tiny vegetable and nut biscuits. The gentleman introduced himself as Mr Chaddar and we also met his wife and ten-year-old son who served us the nibbles. These were followed by several glasses of brandy. Mr Chaddar's English was very good and he explained a route to us which hopefully would avoid the swollen rivers.

At one point in the conversation the son was sent out into the street. He returned a few minutes later and our host asked us to go to the door. If his English hadn't been so good we might have thought he was asking us to leave, but no, his son had been sent to fetch the local snake charmer to entertain us! After this we were told that lunch was about to be served and we were taken to another room in the house where the table was set for three. Mrs Chaddar and son were not eating but waited on us at the table. Thank goodness we had done our homework. We were not offered any cutlery but an endless supply of *pooris*, which are rather like individual Yorkshire puddings and are served very fresh and warm. You use them to carry the vegetables and potato mixture from the central dish to your own small dish and then to your mouth, using your right hand only, of course.* There was also a salad dish made up of onions, chillies and tomatoes. We had

---

* You use your left hand to clean yourself after using the toilet and therefore it has negative connotations. It is appreciated if you make the effort to use only your right hand. I was actually handed a book by a teacher in a very crowded classroom with the words 'please excuse my left hand'.

a slight problem when the chillies caused us to cough and poor Mrs Chaddar was reprimanded by her husband for not removing the strong chillies for the guests, but there was ample water to quench the fire. The first course was followed by a type of rice pudding. We did have spoons for this, but I still kept my left hand in my trouser pocket in case I inadvertently offended these charming people. I was shown into the kitchen after lunch, which was like a workroom rather than just a kitchen. I was there to be shown the sewing and embroidery that Mrs Chaddar was working on. This gave me the opportunity to glance around to find that the other family members were having their lunch from what we had not eaten, along with freshly cooked *pooris*. Mrs Chaddar did not speak English but it's surprising what you can find out with smiles and frowns and nods.

It was four o'clock when we excused ourselves, not wanting to be asked to stay to tea as we had eaten and drunk so much. They were a most hospitable family, anxious to treat us as guests in their country, and what a delight they were to meet. I have told this story many times, usually admitting that I have never welcomed strangers in this way. This family perhaps had more to share than some of the poorer families, but it's not the amount on offer but the willingness with which it's given that was so humbling.

A loud knocking on our rest house door woke us at about five o'clock the next morning. It was Mr Chaddar. He had heard by word of mouth that the bridge over the Narmada River was open and his shouts of 'Sahib Wilkinson' accompanied by 'You must go now' got us moving quickly. However, when we reached the bridge it was still under water and obviously damaged. We tried a detour, but only managed twenty miles before being confronted with two feet of water flowing faster than we liked over a small bridge. The second alternative was more successful, thanks to our exhaust extension. As the passenger, I sat with my feet on the dashboard, holding the hose high through the open window while water was coming in around the doors, and Graham as the driver negotiated two bridges, one wooden and one cobbled, not wanting to go too slowly for fear of stalling the engine and cutting out in mid-flow, but neither wanting to go too fast in case a part of the bridge was not there.

A toll bridge eventually took us across the Narmada River. A glance at a map of India will show you that this river must be nearly as big as the Ganges, even though its name meant little to us. It flows from Madhya Pradesh to its mouth north of Bombay, about two thirds of the way across the whole country. The town of Bhopal, unknown to us then but now well known since the devastating chemical explosion in 1984, was off to the east as we continued via Deshgagon and Burhampur to Edladabad where we found a rest house for the night. We had decided that we would have to forgo Bombay (now called Mumbai) to keep ourselves on schedule for the boat from Madras. We were now not using the AA route prepared for us, which meant we were not sure of accommodation or fuelling stops, but we managed.

Some tourist time was called for after the headache of floods so we decided to visit the Ajanta caves – Buddhist temples dating from the second century BC, dug out of a steep cliff. Until the seventh century AD, the monks lived in their community here, carving the cliff into a Buddhist shrine. In addition to the statues chipped out of the rock, the walls of the caves are painted, telling the story of Buddha as well as giving us details of life at the time. We looked at four of the twenty-nine caves. How do you choose which to see? You rely on the locals. A friendly young man attached himself to us, insisting he carried our small bag, which had not been let out of our sight. Indeed, Graham actually slept every night with it under his pillow, his thinking being that any thief would wake him trying to steal it. Our passports and money were now in the care of our guide who took us to see the best of the frescoes in caves one, two, seventeen and nineteen, where the best sculptures were also to be found. The main sculpture in cave one is a huge Buddha, while cave seventeen contains a gallery of paintings that have not been too badly damaged by time or by the water which covered the caves until the early 1800s. There is so much to see here that you always run out of time. Perhaps your brain can only take in so much anyway. You need to visit it for yourself, really. I hope it hasn't been made too touristy over the past thirty years.

We spent that night at a rest house at Chausala, for which we paid seven and a half rupees – who needs the AA's list of places to stay? We then drove on to link up with the NH9 to Hyderabad. We did not know that there was a horse-race meeting in the city – we missed that in our guidebooks although it was there – therefore there was no accommodation anywhere at 5 p.m. We did manage to cash a traveller's cheque at a hotel and so were able to leave the city. Well, we tried to leave. There were no signposts and so we were forced to ask directions at almost every junction. This is tricky when you think the town you want to head for is called Mahaboodnagass! Our compass at least told us we were going vaguely south and we eventually found the NH7.

Just checking no bits of bridge washed away.

We decided that the worst of the flood problems were behind us as we encountered no swollen rivers on our way to the overnight stop at the cheapest accommodation yet, in a traveller's bungalow at Shadnagar. We were charged two rupees. The water was brought up for us in large clay pots from the bottom of a rather steep hill and we settled in for the evening, cooking our meal on our little portable gas stoves. A new experience awaited us when there was a knock on the door and another couple stood there, requesting to use our bathroom to refresh themselves. This seemed to be standard procedure. Imagine if this were to happen in your English hotel, you'd be a little puzzled, no doubt claiming that you had paid for the room, etc. but we went with the flow. The gentleman, a bank official, spoke good English. Again, we met the hospitality that we were recognising as an Indian trait. While his wife was freshening up, he gave us his phone number in case we needed assistance in any way. We told him we were hoping to look up a contact in Bangalore and he immediately said he would call on this contact and tell him we were on our way and should arrive in Bangalore in a few days. When they had left, the caretaker had to replenish our water supply; this was of course done very willingly.

We were in southern India and after leaving Hyderabad the road signs were now displayed in three languages – Hindi, English and what we presumed was Tamil. There were several large quarries and lots of big rocks strewn along the NH7 – at random, we thought, until we saw the road gangs at intervals still chipping away at the rocks. Some of the houses in the bigger towns had stone-built walls, but the villages now were smaller without the roadside stalls we had got used to seeing, and with some houses built from sticks and leaves and bullock dung. There were lots of rice fields on this stretch although, in contrast to the lands further north, lots of the river beds were dry. It was in this area that we saw a steam train at a small village station taking water on board from an overhead tank. It took a few minutes for us to realise that the long queue of women were collecting hot, steamy water as it belched from the engine. They then walked away with the large pots of water on the heads to do the washing nearby; was this the equivalent of the English launderette?

We only had one more night, at Penukonda, before reaching Bangalore about midday. We found the post and telegraph office and put in a phone call to the shipping company in Madras confirming the sailing date to Malaysia as 18 September. The Tourist Information Office, which we found in Mahatma Gandhi Road, contacted the YWCA and booked a room for us. We found a bookshop and bought a map of the town and also some cornflakes from a chemist shop called Spencer's. Although rather expensive at over six rupees for a small packet, we had to force ourselves to eat these as they were not made by Kellogg's! Our first impression of Bangalore was of wide streets, with trees and several parks. Now the city is known as the IT capital of India, and may well be the place you are connected to via a call centre.

Before leaving England, a colleague had given us the address of the YWCA and the name of the lady responsible for the guest house. The rooms there are usually occupied by young single girls in employment or education in the city. But, like most of the accommodation in India, the rooms could also be used by bona fide travellers. That evening we met Mavis Ramsbotham, with whom we have corresponded since and whom I met again thirty years later. Having got this far safely, we now felt we could really relax for a few days before proceeding to the shipping port of Madras. Relaxation for Graham was only possible after he had given the van a comprehensive service, which included relining the brakes as well as retightening all the loose screws once more. We visited the local supermarket for a few supplies, but our accommodation at this hostel did include breakfast. This was a milky type of noodles/spaghetti, a banana and a cup of tea, for which we paid two rupees in addition to the payment for the room. The rooms all led off a central dining/sitting area. At the rear of our room was our bathroom, which had an outside door where the houseboy appeared in the mornings with a large container of hot water. A tap on the wall at a height of about three feet provided cold water when the supply was on and served as a shower. The metal bedsteads were supplied with mosquito nets as well as horsehair mattresses and bedlinen. Most of the rooms had several beds and the girls staying there shared in groups of about six. Our friend Mavis had a small room of her own and one of the servant ladies spent the nights on a mat across the doorway of the room. She was a member of the lowest caste. It is due to Gandhi and subsequent legislation that 'untouchables' no longer exist in law, but this was the phrase still being used at this time.

The banker gentleman we had met was as good as his word; a second contact came to the hostel that evening, having been told of our arrival. The use of a house had been arranged for us as long as we wished. The owners were still at their hill-station home, a leftover location from when the British found the heat of the plains unbearable and retreated to more mountainous regions. We arranged to meet Eric at his home the next day, but spent the evening with Mavis, who took us to see a procession, part of a local religious festival which was deliberately multi-faith. Bangalore had definite areas for Hindus and Muslims as well as Catholic Christians and the Church of South India. We were told that the Muslim community always made a big effort to compensate for previous antagonism. It certainly seemed as if the world and his wife were out that night!

It would be good to have space in which to spread out. We found Cooketown, a suburb of Bangalore, and met Eric as arranged. The caretaker, who was called Joeboy, helped us unload the van and then summoned his wife and friend to clean the house for us while we were taken to Eric's home to meet his family. We had heard that there might be an introduction of petrol rationing, so we filled the tank that afternoon. Having travelled so far, lack of petrol would be a ridiculous reason for missing our boat.

Meeting Joeboy and his family this day was the beginning of thirty years correspondence between our two families. As head of his family, Joeboy worked six days a week for the post office, and was very proud of this, earning four hundred rupees a month. He had seven children, the youngest being only weeks old. They lived in a two-room hut at the rear of our big house, for which his rent was fifty rupees. He also paid out forty rupees a month in school fees for his children at an English-speaking school. This was not the total fees, but he supplemented this by doing sewing repairs for the school on his ancient Singer treadle sewing machine. This machine and his radio were his prized possessions.

Mrs Joeboy cooked for the family outside the house in the shelter of the house wall. She came each morning with the baby strapped to her back to clean our house. Once, I managed to persuade her in sign language that this was not necessary, but the other days she quietly insisted. We felt it was important to her to complete her duties and so we left her in the house to do the chores.

I spent one day in the school at the YWCA. The school was then for three- to nine-year-old children of all religions. Lessons were taught in English. The youngest class for children aged three to five had fifty-two children whereas the oldest class only had nine children. I found the children all eager to learn and the older ones wanted to know about England. We spent some time with a world globe, the only resource available. This lack of equipment is still very evident thirty years later.

While I was enjoying myself at the school, Graham was doing his best to service Eric's 1952 Morris Minor. Fortunately, some of our spare parts were suitable because this saloon seemed to be held together by mud and good luck. In return we were taken out to lunch to Tom's Café, where we were advised to have chicken biryani with curried lamb sauce. This seemed a popular place as it was a large restaurant, but full and busy. Over the next couple of days we were shown the city of Bangalore, including the Lal Bagh Gardens and Cubbon Park. We were invited to the children's assembly with which they start their school day. We stood there feeling quite important as they marched past us into school, each one giving us a beaming smile and saying, 'Good morning, Auntie' or 'Good morning, Uncle' as they walked into lessons.

Eventually we had to move on to Madras. We repacked the van, took lots of photos and said lots of thank yous. We left Bangalore about midday, spending just one night before Madras at a PWD inspection bungalow in Baluchettychatnan for the grand price of one and a half rupees (less than ten pence). The following morning our usual early start paid off. Here we were, approaching the outskirts of Madras around 9.30 a.m. The sense of pride in our achievement, together with a huge feeling of relief, was apparent by the wide grins on our faces as we located the YWCA hostel and booked ourselves in.

The importance of reaching this stage in our travels, safely and on time, had been constantly in our thoughts since leaving England. We had made the port of shipment for the last leg of our journey and it was someone else's turn to navigate and drive! After the long weeks and miles on the road, we could now look forward to six days at sea relaxing and preparing mentally for our time in Malaysia, to be followed by a second boat trip before the trek across Australia from Fremantle to Melbourne, our final destination.

We had a few days before the SS *Rajula* sailed, but we needed to visit the shipping agents in the city to complete the paperwork. The usual helpful local turned up at our side in the shipping office; he seemed to know we would be arriving. He introduced himself as Mr T Krishna Rao, an agent who was known to the company, and we were happy for him to help us complete the documentation required. The van had to be weighed, which meant a drive through a maze of city streets to the weighbridge. Mr Rao was in the passenger seat as I squeezed into the back. The vehicle also had to be measured in length as the shipping costs were based on this. We visited a nearby bank to organise a cheque for the freight charge, having already paid the passenger fares in London. We had got used to the length of time formalities took and it was now late afternoon, but it was with relief that we paid Mr Rao his fee and left him to finalise the paperwork after arranging to meet him three days later at the agent's office for loading instructions. We were very trusting!

It was not long after returning to the hostel in the early evening that the first of many local people knocked on our room's door asking if we had any spare parts to sell. Word travels fast when a British Morris arrives in town! People came, hoping to get their own vehicles moving again by buying spark plugs, or even make them a little safer by buying our spare brake linings. Windscreen wiper blades, a spare tyre and other spare parts were also bartered for. By the end of our stay here, the stock of spares was looking rather depleted. There were strict rules about importing spare parts into the country, but who was to say we hadn't used them? We were getting low on cash by then! We were working on the assumption that the nearer we got to our destination, the less important our own need was.

We spent time sorting out the van and doing the usual routine checks. We also rearranged all our belongings, stowing as much as possible under the false floor. The grounds of the hostel were very shaded and the vehicles were parked in a pleasant area where we sat in the evenings, sharing experiences with other overlanders, able to help each other with first-hand advice.

The southern marina around Mount Road was a very clean and impressive part of Madras. We also visited the university and the art gallery during these leisurely couple of days. There was a

Church of South India within walking distance of the hostel and I decided to attend the evening service on the Sunday before we left. It is an indication of the feeling of safety we experienced in India that I was quite at ease walking the short distance alone and our logbook stated that at no time did we feel threatened or uncomfortable in this country.

Only struts and nets were used to load the vehicles!

The day for loading our van had arrived; we had arranged to meet the agent at the shipping office, Binneys, at two o'clock. Five vehicles went in convoy to the wharf where they were subjected to a customs check before being loaded on board the SS *Rajula* around five o'clock. Our hearts were in our mouths as we watched the van craned onto the sixty-eight-year-old boat. It was then out of our hands and we returned to the YWCA hostel by taxi with our overland friends. Even the journey there was an experience, as the driver changed gear straight from first to top – he didn't seem to have the ones in between; not that we could help, a spare gearbox was one part we did not have.

Having lost our vehicles, all the overlanders decided to dine in at the hostel. This was our last night on land for a week before the cruise ahead. It was a noisy evening meal but not a late one as we had a taxi booked for the morning. With our on-board suitcases in hand, we left for the wharf. This taxi didn't have an obvious problem with the gearbox, he didn't use gears much, but his foot seemed to be permanently stuck on the accelerator; this meant two lads had their arms through the open windows holding the suitcases onto the roof rack which was held on with a couple of rusty bolts and some thick string! Compared with the lengthy procedure for the vehicle, our formalities were a doddle; our suitcases were carried and we had to do a hurried walk to keep up with the porters as they led us on board for what we learned was to be the last voyage for the ship across the Bay of Bengal. She had been bought by the Indian government and was to be used for coastal work and later to repatriate forces serving in Bangladesh, as we now know it.

Malaysia/Singapore

*A*LTHOUGH WE DIDN'T LEAVE MADRAS HARBOUR UNTIL LATE afternoon there was plenty of entertainment for us after we had eaten lunch. The intervening hours were spent watching the boat filling up with about eight hundred Indians who were accommodated on the aft and forward decks. These passengers were on their way to Malaysia and Singapore for work, each paying about eighteen pounds for a single fare. Some found space in the hold of the ship, using the metal cots and wooden beds provided; those on deck cooked their own food and slept on their own mats. There were only forty-six European cabin passengers.

At last it was time to open our suitcases, packed all those weeks ago in London especially for our two stretches of cruise time. After all the trouble we had taken to have respectable clean clothes for this part of our travels, we discovered that everything was covered in red dust. We had hand washed our other clothes all along our route and I'm rather ashamed to say we didn't always do a very good job. The white shirts were a distinct shade of grey, even when supposedly freshly laundered. One local lady had washed for us and she had handed our shirts back to us beautifully white and ironed – and very thin! Fortunately on board ship there were facilities for us to wash and iron our dust-laden best attire.

Our first night on board was somewhat exciting as we headed south towards Nagapattinam through a heavy sea. With the sound of seasickness in our ears, plus the smell, we were forced to close the porthole in our cabin early in the evening. Unfortunately, it overlooked the rear of the ship where several hundred of our Indian passengers were accommodated on the deck and hatch covers. We had purposefully booked a cabin with a porthole, but were disappointed that it faced the rear and not the side as we had anticipated.

The SS *Rajula* was a lovely British India steam ship of around

9,000 tons, with British officers and Indian crew; a beautiful old lady of the sea who had seen decades of service in this part of the world. The food on board was wonderful, too. When we anchored off Nagapattinam early the next morning, all the cabin passengers seemed to be present at breakfast, despite the night's rough session. Like us, the other overlanders had been careful with their food supplies latterly and were ready for large quantities of home-cooked fare. Bacon and eggs for breakfast was a bonus – all cooked over coal. The on-board catering was first class with a varied selection at each meal and plenty of it. This was after being woken at six o'clock to be served 'tiffin' – a cup of tea with a plate of bread and butter.

Our cabin was very spacious, with a washbasin and enough hanging and drawer space for two. Instead of the usual bunks we were expecting, we had two single metal beds or cots. These were not fastened down and spent their time sliding around the cabin floor. However, Graham's didn't move quite so much if he was in it as ballast! There were shower and toilet facilities nearby on the same deck. Perhaps you are now realising that I use the word 'cruise' rather loosely and should perhaps say 'time spent at sea'.

While at anchor, the ship was a hive of activity with small sailing boats pulling alongside to offload bags of onions; we apparently took sixty tons on board together with another six hundred Indian deck passengers. We steamed straight back into a storm with heavy rain and rough seas when we left Nagapattinam late in the evening. We still kept our porthole closed!

The next four days were uneventful; the sea was now calm and smooth and all the European passengers were in relaxed mood, enjoying playing table tennis, lazing on the reclining deckchairs, reading or chatting. We had the odd film show on deck at night: Indian films with English subtitles. Graham did join a tour of the engine room when invited by the chief engineer, only to wish he had declined as the heat down below was unbearable, not to mention the deafening noise.

Although we arrived off Penang by breakfast time, the ship was in quarantine until tea; it took this time for our health documents to be checked. As we were cabin passengers we got priority. The immigration officers who came on board were very badly mannered and most unwelcoming, rather a shock to the system; we had got used to our presence being appreciated wherever we had been up to now! However, compared to some of our acquaintances we were lucky, being given a two-week stopover visa for Malaysia with the probability of an extension. Some of the other passengers were only allowed one or two weeks non-extendable. It is important to remember that in the 1970s overlanders were treated with a degree of suspicion, being viewed as possible hippies, particularly if sporting long hair. We had made a point of being fairly well presented when interviewed by the immigration officials and perhaps that's why we were given a two-week extendable visa. I said cabin passengers were interviewed first, but we were still near the desk when one of the first of the deck passengers was suddenly marched to one side and handcuffed to a nearby table. We were told he had a forged passport and no ticket.

We docked at Georgetown on Penang Island in the early evening, but the vehicles could not be unloaded until the onions had been taken off. We were able to go ashore and look around the town. We had a rather disturbed night, not only as we were not being rocked to sleep by the gentle movement we had got used to, but also because we checked every couple of hours to see if the unloading of the vehicles was in progress. Eventually this happened after breakfast.

Shortly afterwards, a quiet prayer of thanks was said on the wharf. Three out of the five overlanders' vehicles had been broken into when in the hold of the boat but ours was not one of them. It was now we were grateful that Graham had fitted bars on the back windows and curtained off the rear of our van to block any view of what was inside. Our van was unloaded minus just one mud flap, but it had acquired a strong smell of onions!

Soon after unloading, Graham walked into Georgetown to begin the procedure for clearing the vehicle from the wharf: third-party insurance, customs office, shipping agents and port authority. Because of the mishap on the voyage, I stayed with the other car owners to take turns watching the vehicles now sitting on the dockside. Although we had been officially in Malaysia for nearly two days, it was getting towards dusk when we eventually cleared customs to travel north around Penang Island.

We had driven as far as the eleventh milepost when we spotted a beautiful place to pitch tents, ten metres from the water's edge, under the palm trees – coconut palms, actually, and several coconuts came down very close to our tent! It was also near to a large but empty hotel. After a chat with the management, we obtained permission to use their facilities for fifty Malaysian cents per day. What a great spot it was to camp! We immediately got back in the van to find our overland friends who joined us at this dream location.

We all spent a few days enjoying the beautiful setting and swimming in the warm water. Three out of the five couples had to sort out repairs to windscreens and forced door or window locks, needing time to unwind and put that part of the journey behind them. We found a local shop for supplies where the shopkeeper was very friendly, with a good stock of essential foodstuffs. We mostly bought flour and bananas and seemed to cook an endless supply of banana pancakes. This was supplemented with freshly caught fish bought in a nearby village. Our stay here included visits at night to some of the kampongs where we watched the men fishing with nets by hand in the bay as well as from boats a little further out. We were fascinated by their simple houses on stilts in villages which seemed to accommodate a mixture of races – Malay, Chinese as well as Indian and European. Above all, we were privileged every evening to witness the most beautiful sunset. What a life!

We did make an excursion to the Snake Temple, built in 1850 by a Chinese priest as a sanctuary for snakes, which are believed to be the disciples of the god Chor Soo Kong. The snakes are a variety known as Wagler pit vipers which have a highly toxic venom. Although they were coiling around the altar and other parts of the temple, they seemed pretty docile. We also found a supermarket in Penang Road that sold European food, so we stocked up a little, prior to moving on to the mainland.

With our stay at Batu Ferringhi nearly over, we all decided on a farewell barbeque on the beach before going our separate ways. Everyone contributed something to cook – fish, pineapple, bananas, potatoes and even Walls sausages! As well as tea to drink,

Graham and I donated two bottles of Turkish wine originally destined for friends in Australia. I have not yet found a more beautiful spot for a barbeque.

We couldn't cross to the mainland without visiting the Thai temple with its famous reclining Buddha – a statue over one hundred feet long covered in gold leaf. Impressive as it is, the local people are still able to rent niches of the hollow plinth to rest ashes of their dead family members there. After visiting the immigration office – where, true to their word, the officials gave us our visa extension – another short sea trip on the ferry to Butterworth and the mainland was the order of the day.

We had decided to visit the Cameron Highlands on mainland Malaysia and so drove along a winding road through jungle interspersed with waterfalls. The villages of Ipoh and Topah came and went as we climbed higher for thirty-seven miles. Although narrow, the road surface was good. On reaching the town of Tanah Rata, we camped free of charge in the grounds of the rest house, with permission to use their bathroom. Our evening meal that night was at a local Muslim-owned café recommended to us by some travellers we got chatting to. Money was getting rather short, so we chose about the cheapest item on the menu, rotis with chicken curry sauce plus very sweet tea. This didn't break the bank as the grand total was less than twenty pence, or one Malaysian dollar.

The next day we decided to take a jungle walk on one of the recognised trails and it turned out to be a fascinating trek. We were on the floor of the jungle, so it was humid and very dim; the sun hardly penetrated through the overhead canopy. It was a real test of our eyesight to spot the wildlife. We could hear so many strange sounds and see an abundance of coloured flowers. We found our way without any problem, as there was only the one track through otherwise thick undergrowth.

It was along here that we literally bumped into a small group of locals. We thought they must be heading home to their village with packs of supplies. We tried a conversation in a mixture of broken English, sign language and my attempts at Malay, that is 'Salamat pagi', meaning good morning. Eventually it appeared that they were inviting us to accompany them to their village. We were tempted but the problem was that it was a further two days' walking, so we politely declined their kind offer. Our day's walk had given us an appetite, so we splashed out that night at the same café but tried something different; we wished we hadn't. Our small dishes were filled from the large communal bowl on display on a side table, which was no problem. Our rotis were freshly cooked, tasted faintly of coconut and were lovely. We were disappointed with the lamb curry as it seemed to be lamb bones rather than meat. We were eating in the same way as the locals, using our teeth to scrape the small pieces of flesh from the bones. It wasn't until we were paying the bill, of nearly two Malaysian dollars, that we realised why the curry was all bones; both our table and the adjoining one where a group of local men had been eating were cleared. The remnants of the meal were of course bones, as the only inedible ingredient, and these were tipped back into the communal dish, to be served yet again to the next customer. We tried a different restaurant the next night!

Before leaving the Cameron Highlands we paid a visit to a nearby tea plantation – the Boh estate. We toured the factory, learning the difference between the broken orange pekoe and the sweepings and all grades in between. Samples were given us to try, of course. A drive through the plantation showed us the workers, women again, picking the small new leaves from the bushes that covered every bit of ground, often on a steep slope so as not to waste any soil. We also checked out the houses built for the families on the estate. We got the impression that they were quite well looked after by the employers.

This part of Malaysia was still the hill country where the wealthy British and their families would have retreated when the heat and humidity were too much for them. The downpours of rain could be very sudden and heavy, but the air would be refreshed when, just as suddenly, the rain would stop. We had to follow the road downhill back to Topah and on to the main road to Tanyong and a few other small places with difficult names to Western ears, before climbing again up to Frazer's Hill. Here we camped in a picnic area known as the Glen. The names seem to imply links with the British. A local man insisted on helping us find the camping spot by running up the road in front of the van for several miles, in case we inadvertently drove past; it was small and surrounded by a dense covering of trees and bushes. He lived higher up still and stopped the following morning to speak to us as he walked back down the hill to work. Whether he was checking we were safe or trying out his English I don't know, but I can't see me running for two or three miles to show a complete stranger a camp spot.

Our early morning call had been very early so we were on the road to Kuantan in good time before heading north along the coast to Kuala Dungan. We had been told about a turtle beach ten miles further north at Rantua Abang. I watched a holiday programme on television recently featuring this spot and I'm really glad I saw it thirty years ago.

Another super spot to spend a few days.

We rented a hut here as our van was parked a little way off the dunes that blocked the way to the turtle area. Our choice of hut was the economy type at two Malaysian dollars per night, with a sand floor, a very large wooden sleeping platform and a stand for an oil lamp. As the door had a big gap at the bottom, we often found chickens in our room, maybe trying to escape their turn in the pot. We were travelling to a budget and the cost of a deluxe room, i.e. a concrete floor, was three dollars and still came with resident chickens! The next couple of days were spent swimming, eating and sleeping. The café proprietor was very trusting. We were invited to help ourselves to cold drinks during the day and to pay him in the evening. On the menu there was chicken (surprise!), fish, rice and green beans plus a milky Milo drink before bed. Bedtime on our first night was not until the early hours of the morning but – alas – no turtles came ashore to lay their eggs. There were protected hatchery areas along the miles of beach.

I guess the turtle beach was on the 'must visit' list as our overland friends all turned up during the next few days. We still had not had seen a turtle, despite staying up till 3 a.m. and walking miles along the beach with our torches. The closest to a sighting was turtle footprints. It was not to be. The turtle season runs from May till September – we were just a little too late to witness these extraordinary giant turtles from the South China Sea which visit the beaches of western Malaysia annually.

Reluctantly we left Rantua Abang, heading south along the coast road. Two free river crossings by ferry and one toll bridge brought us towards Mersing. We spent one night in a really quiet spot next to the boathouse belonging to a motel, but the next night enquiries at the rest house near the town led us to make camp on the golf course. This was close to the sea, but the frogs must like the salt air as they made their croaking noise for most of the night.

Driving towards Kota Tingi brought us into rubber country. We stopped at a plantation to watch the workers – that is, the women, of course – collecting the liquid from the small cups attached to the trees. This liquid rubber was poured into large rectangular moulds and, when solid enough to handle, the thick slabs were pressed through an ancient hand mangle before being rolled again with large rolling pins. These sheets were then hung up to dry. The process, though fascinating to watch for a while, seemed rather labour intensive. Perhaps some of the passengers from the *Rajula* would find employment here.

Leaving the plantation, we headed for Lambong to see the

waterfalls situated along the slopes to Gunong Muntahak. The falls are about three hundred feet above sea level and are immediately below the catchment area which supplies the water to Kota Tinggi. The day was very warm, so we enjoyed swimming in the pool below the falls before retracing our steps a little to pick up the main road to Johore Baharu. We had to be very careful here; we knew we did not have permission to drive into Singapore. At the third attempt we found the rest house on the seafront road without getting on the causeway which only leads to Singapore. Four of our friends turned up at this rest house.

The accommodation here turned out to be the mustering point for the overlanders, enabling us to complete shipping formalities. If the Malaysian authorities were unwelcoming, well, I'm not sure how to describe the Singaporeans. The strict conditions meant we could only travel into Singapore on public transport. Our own vehicles could only be driven in on the day of departure for Australia. We needed to travel into Singapore to check departure dates and also to see if we could change our booking for an earlier crossing. The authorities at the border gave us a one-day pass enabling us to catch a bus and then taxi to the Anglo-French travel offices. They were the agents for Austasia line with whom we hoped to find berths and van space. Our luck was in. They offered us two berths in separate four-berth cabins and space for the van sailing on the SS *Malaysia* in two days' time. Fortunately, after an hour in the offices of Blue Funnel Line, our passage money was transferred. What would we have done without the AA? Visits to their offices gave us an export permit for the van and completed the documentation with a visit to the freight division for payment. It was a busy day, but a successful one. Just one hiccup – money. It was not possible to use an ATM in those dark ages, but Barclays Bank seemed to come to our rescue. A branch had opened on 1 September, just the previous month. We thought we had managed to transfer some money from our London account to a bank in Perth, Western Australia. Unfortunately it didn't arrive. Of course, we didn't know this at the time, so we returned to the Malaysian side of the border that evening pretty pleased with ourselves.

The next day was rather hectic. Some of our friends were not quite as short of cash as we were and had a room at the rest house while we were camping in the grounds. In exchange for the use of their shower we cooked banana pancakes for six hungry people, between visiting the post office for last minute poste restante and packing the van very carefully and even more discreetly than last time to discourage thieves.

Ample time to reach the docks was allowed the following morning as we proceeded towards the causeway. We anticipated trouble with some officials somewhere. However, apart from the Malaysian customs and police not knowing what to do with the vehicle documents, departing from that country was no problem. Singapore – well! There were three vehicles lined up together. We were going for the safety-in-numbers tactics. We sat before the desk while one immigration official walked slowly around us, possibly inspecting length of hair! Then they wanted to give us a police escort to the wharf, with an official travelling in one of the vehicles. There was, of course, no room in any of the three, and at the suggestion that one of us should travel in by bus there was an outcry from all six of us. Eventually, after taking our passports away for a while to another office and filling in John and Paul's details on our vehicle carnet, we were given a special pass to travel unescorted on a direct route to the docks. A phone call from the police to the wharf ensured they were on the lookout for our arrival by ten o'clock. Customs stamped our Carnet de Passage into the country and the good AA stamped us out as we made it at the wharf by 10 a.m. for loading. They were waiting for us, but the customs check to depart the country was non-existent. We sailed within ten minutes of loading the vehicles and ourselves, even though it was now evening. Perhaps it was because we had been so well treated in the Asian countries that we felt unwelcome in Singapore. Perhaps it was because this was a wealthier country than those we had travelled through since leaving Europe and we certainly were not in the 'rich tourist' category that we felt we were not wanted there. Not that we were given much opportunity to contribute to their economy. Or perhaps it was just the hippy ideas of the 1970s that the Singapore authorities did not want to encourage.

Australia

THE STRETCH AT SEA LASTED EIGHT DAYS AND THIS SHIP *WAS* a cruise vessel. Our best attire was scarcely comparable with that of the other passengers. However, our credibility improved when the other passengers chatted to us and so learned of our venture. Apart from a brief stop in Indonesia where we visited the capital, Djakarta, we were more than happy just to keep going on nearer to our goal. Whether we were travel weary I'm not sure, but the usual on-board activities were just time fillers until the landfall dinner off Fremantle in late October. This, for us, was a mini celebration of a safe and successful end to a trip across the world by road. We had made Australia. The fact that we still had to drive more than two-thousand miles across Australia, including over the Nullarbor Plain, seemed immaterial really!

Although we docked in the early morning, our vehicle was not unloaded until the evening. It was then immediately impounded on the wharf to await formalities the following day. We spent a comfortable night at a nearby hotel and headed for the bank at opening time to collect the money arranged back in Singapore. Alas, no cash. However, we were now in a country where the telephone network was efficient and there were no language problems and really we were not causing much interest for anyone else. We weren't even offered a cup of tea while arrangements were made for Graham's parents to authorise payment of some money from their account. We arranged temporary car insurance which enabled us to travel from the wharf area to the nearby quarantine station for the van to be steam cleaned. I believe Australian regulations on importing foodstuff/vegetable matter are still rigorous, even travelling from state to state within the country, and who knew what our vehicle might have been carrying. We were allowed through customs, got clearance from the shipping agents and the port authorities, and all that remained was a trip to the police station. Here the roadworthy inspection was carried out and we arranged more permanent third-party car insurance for driving within Australia. Formalities completed a little quicker than in Malaysia, we drove until late into the evening when we stopped in a tourist information bay for the night near Coolgardie. The road across the Nullarbor in those days was rough to say the least, hard-going and very dusty – just what we had got used to since leaving Europe really. Those travelling the same route today have a bitumen road with roadhouses at intervals and landing strips for the flying-doctor service for any emergency that may occur. About the only stop for a meal on the Nullarbor in 1973 was a place called Ivy Tanks. Desperate for a feed after a long, hard day at the wheel, we sampled the food at this middle-of-nowhere stop.

The drinks are more important than the food.

Sadly for us, the flies outnumbered the soggy warm chips and sausages by about a thousand to one. The cold beer was good though.

The next overnight stop at Mundranbilla had us getting closer to the South Australian border, not that this involved anything other than a road sign telling us – no passport control or teenager lads with automatic rifles! We travelled nearly three hundred miles of rough roads the following day as far as Penong, before we camped at Ceduna after a long, tiring day on the road. We were now well into South Australia, but a petrol tanker drivers' strike made our next day rather stressful as we felt obliged to keep the fuel tank filled at every opportunity. A feeling of déjà vu came over us. However, we made it to Murray Bridge for our last overnight stop on the road. Our goal had nearly been reached, just the state of Victoria now and then our destination: Melbourne.

The adrenaline was pumping as we expected the day's run to be the last. Even if we hadn't been used to early starts, we would still have been on the move by six o'clock. No doubt Graham's parents were getting excited too; an emotion to replace the worries they had been feeling since we had left England. London to Melbourne, what an epic drive that still seems! At last, the end loomed near. It was the longest, hardest road journey I've ever attempted, but also the most fascinating and rewarding one.

We reached Graham's parents' home twelve hours after breaking camp that morning. Our total drive had been 11,713 miles through seventeen countries over fourteen weeks.

Looking Back

*M*Y MEMORY IS A PARADOX; I CAN REMEMBER THE EVENTS clearly, tens of years ago and yet it seems much more recent than that. Looking at all the happenings since that journey, of course it's a lifetime ago. But that trip definitely had a lasting influence on my life. On a very basic level, just to see first hand the countries that were only known as names on a map or pictures in a book was an eye-opener. Today's young people have the benefits of modern technology and direct communication via messaging and webcams, but even that cannot compete with face-to-face contact, atmosphere and the *wow* factor. I do not think experiencing the majesty of a mosque in Iran can possibly be bettered nor even equalled by anything technology has to offer. How does technology conjure up the smells of the market in Old Delhi?

People today often demand instant results, as in instant messaging on the internet, but on our travels we saw a different reaction to time; patience and attention were given to us as guests, the time taken to treat us as welcome visitors was given willingly. We hoped that the contacts we had arranged prior to setting out would be amicable towards us, but nothing prepared us for the support and friendliness we received from complete strangers. We learned patience as we experienced the transport and the meals and the language for ourselves. The importance attached to the learning of English was evident in several of the countries we passed through, from wanting to practise English conversation with us to willingly paying higher fees for the children to attend an English-speaking school. In India there seemed to be a genuine affection between the local people and the British, irrespective of the previous struggle for their independence against the colonialists.

At the time of writing, there are reports of conflict in Nepal, with more than one hundred thousand people demonstrating on the streets in the capital, Kathmandu. Albert, the Australian bus, finished his trip in that city. This aggression has been in the news intermittently for some time, but has been overshadowed by events in Iraq and Afghanistan because of the British troops involved in those conflicts. Then we hear of disagreements regarding Iran's nuclear enrichment programme.

Compared with major international situations, my personal involvement is very minor. I know my work as a primary teacher benefited from this long trek; my own personal interest in other cultures has been carried through in my teaching, especially in the areas of geography, religious education and English as an acquired language. First-hand incidents have kept classes interested. I have kept in contact both with the school and YWCA in Bangalore and also with Mr Joeboy and family. Sadly Mr Joeboy himself died some years ago, but since then the letters have been written by one of the children. We sent money each year until their letters told us it wasn't arriving. So, in 2004, I decided to visit them again. Accompanied by a friend who was also a teacher, we stayed at the YWCA hostel, where very little had changed during the intervening years. We actually had the same room in the hostel; I don't think it was the same houseboy who brought our morning hot water, but otherwise the bathroom arrangements had not changed at all. The same metal bedsteads and horsehair mattresses were still there, as were the resident biting insects! The bites were more common as the mosquito nets from yesteryear were no longer in use.

However, one difference was the presence of a television set in what had been a large entrance area. As I have mentioned, Bangalore is often referred to by the media as the IT capital of the world. It seemed in a small way to have penetrated even this modest hostel. The biggest difference, though, was the growth of that small school at the YWCA; it was amazing. Over the years, the numbers have increased to over one thousand pupils. I had been receiving annual updates on their progress in exam results and those continuing to higher education, but was not prepared for the confidence and high expectations, especially of the older pupils. 'Auntie, I would like to work in medicine... I want to go to university and study for an MBA...' High standards of work were evident throughout the school and this despite the lack of resources: classroom walls were bare, books very few, children paid for their own writing equipment. Academic work is balanced by high standards of work in the arts, as was evidenced by the performances held especially for us. The younger pupils were able to chat confidently about their work and the older ones asked pertinent questions about the curriculum in schools in England.

My donation given to the head teacher was only a drop in the ocean towards resources, but between us we decided to buy some shelving to keep the children's lunch boxes off the floor and away from the ants, and to pay the fees for a child who would be withdrawn from the school as her father had been killed in an accident and her mother could only contribute ten pence towards the monthly fees. I hope my parcels of wallcharts and storybooks have helped to brighten up the nursery classroom.

Catching up after all these years with Mavis and the head teacher of the school and, of course, the children, was the highlight of our visit. The years had not diminished Mavis' matriarchal hold on the hostel and its residents. The other delightful reunion was with Joeboy's family. Mrs Joeboy's English had progressed over the years, enough for me to have a short telephone conversation to arrange dates and times. We could not have been made more welcome. Modern communication was put to good use as the relatives were contacted by mobile phone, and they all gathered at the family home. No matter what they were doing or what was planned, it was not as important as we were! The English-speaking education of the children was invaluable as we were able to talk to the younger family members. The smiles and laughter said enough for those who couldn't manage the intricacies of English or Hindi or Tamil or even Kannada. I shall only say the time spent with the family was delightful.

I decided that one of the differences between doing that journey years ago and trying it now is that today some of the places en route are considered dangerous places, whereas in the 1970s they were rather unknown places. The worry that family and friends had for us was simply because the countries were little more than names on a map; today we have almost instantaneous pictures of events in distant places; the images may be of natural disasters, but more often they seem to show man inflicting horror on man. It is difficult to believe that the world today is less safe than thirty years ago. Does history teach nothing or is it that people refuse to learn from past events? Of course, there are many people travelling without mishap, whether youngsters, retirees or somewhere in-between. Good news does not make headlines. We only hear the bad things. It is possible to be in the wrong place at the wrong time, as our friends John and Paul discovered from their incident in Turkey. Equally we could have been in a difficult position in countries with whom Britain is in dispute over nuclear capability or territorial waters or attempting to improve the lives of ordinary Afghanis in their country. Do the benefits gained outweigh the worries and the risk of bad events? Would cost today make such a trip prohibitive for most people? In many ways today's travel is much easier. Road conditions and car-repair services must have improved. Even photographic proof of a loved one's safety can be sent instantly from a mobile phone. One of our postcards sent home commented that it was a shame our news took so long to reach the UK as we had more update news to tell before they had received the first card!

Perhaps the traveller would be safe and only those left at home would worry, just as our folks did thirty years ago. Would it be worth giving the family back home the anxiety? You must make up your own mind; I can only say that for Graham and I it was the trip of a lifetime.

Appendix 1: Spare Parts

*T*HIS MAY BE OF INTEREST TO THE MECHANICS AMONG THE readers. With the advice and information issued by BMC Cowley, together with the invaluable knowledge and assistance given by Mr Brown, the following is a list of spares carried on the overland drive.

Fire extinguisher
Tow rope
Tool kit
Lamp
Emergency triangle
Second spare wheel and two further tyres
Foot pump and puncture repair kit
Brake linings, cables, brake fluid and seals, bleed kit
Top and bottom radiator hoses, radweld, radiator cap
Air and oil filters
Headlamp unit, bulb kit and fuses
Distributor cap and rotor, points
Accelerator cable
Water pump repair kit and thermostat
Jerrycan x2, petrol pump, funnel with filter
Engine mounts
Fan belt
Spark plugs
Head gasket
Joint/washer set
Clutch plate
Coil
Wiper blades/arms
Exhaust extension
WD40 and oil
Sheet of Perspex

This comprehensive supply of spares was gathered together over several months, and comprised both new parts and second-hand ones – borrowed and procured.

These parts took up a lot of space, but were felt to be necessary. Some of them were used on our friend's Morris saloon in Bangalore, on what must have been its first comprehensive service for years. And others, as mentioned, did help a few Indians whose names we did not know!

Appendix 2: Costing

$\mathcal{P}$RIOR TO LEAVING ENGLAND WE HAD SPENT £620, but this did include the cost of the vehicle as well as supplies of food/spare parts and all the paperwork. The total shipping costs for passengers and van, including port taxes and the channel crossing to France, came to £508. Petrol amounted to £109. More money was spent in India on fuel than any other country but this only averaged nine and a half pence per litre. The cheapest fuel was in Iran and the most expensive in Germany. Accommodation charges totalled just under £50. It is perhaps unfair to compare costs between the beach in Malaysia, a hotel in Australia and a car park in Pakistan. En route, money was spent on road tolls, local food shopping, family gifts, postage, etc., for a total of just over £100.

Grand total: just under £1400.

Printed in the United Kingdom
by Lightning Source UK Ltd.
134581UK00001B/232-246/P